DESTINATION
TRUTH

DESTINATION
TRUTH

Memoirs of a Monster Hunter

Josh Gates

GALLERY BOOKS

New York London Toronto Sydney New Delhi

G

Gallery Books
A Division of Simon & Schuster, Inc.
1230 Avenue of the Americas
New York, NY 10020

First Gallery Books trade paperback edition October 2011

GALLERY BOOKS and colophon are registered trademarks of Simon & Schuster, Inc.

For information about special discounts for bulk purchases, please contact Simon & Schuster Special Sales at 1-866-506-1949 or business@simonandschuster.com.

The Simon & Schuster Speakers Bureau can bring authors to your live event. For more information or to book an event contact the Simon & Schuster Speakers Bureau at 1-866-248-3049 or visit our website at www.simonspeakers.com.

Designed by Jason Snyder

Manufactured in the United States of America

10   9   8   7   6

Library of Congress Cataloging-in-Publication Data

Gates, Josh.
     Destination truth / Josh Gates. —1st Gallery Books trade pbk. ed.
       p. cm.
     1. Cryptozoology—Juvenile literature. 2. Monsters—Juvenile literature.
3. Animals—Folklore—Juvenile literature. I. Title.
     QL88.3.G38 2012
     001.944—dc23
                                                                        2011025162

ISBN 978-0-7434-9172-3
ISBN 978-1-4391-9042-5 (ebook)

To my father, Lee Gates, and grandfather, Lewis Gates.
Real-deal adventurers.

*"One's destination is never a place,
but a new way of seeing things."*

—HENRY MILLER

"The truth is never pure and seldom simple."

—OSCAR WILDE

"Fortune and glory, kid. Fortune and glory."

—INDIANA JONES

CONTENTS

Foreword

The following is a scattershot account of my tenure over the last four years as a professional vagabond, international monster hunter, and paranormal Hardy Boy. After careening through nearly one hundred countries investigating some of humanity's most enduring myths and legends, I have emerged fundamentally changed by the journey (and probably have a few weird diseases to boot).

This book has been written, in large part, on dirty airport floors, in sweltering jungle huts, and by the firelight of chilly mountain lodges. This very sentence is being penned aboard a sailboat off the icy coast of Antarctica. My journals have served as trusted guides and helped me navigate the dense wilderness of memory.

In several places I've taken geographical liberties, changed a few names to protect the guilty, needlessly slandered several people, misused the word "nascent," and in one instance made something up entirely because it sounded very adventurous in my head.

J.

DESTINATION
TRUTH

1: "We Must Go Back"

Cluj, Romania, 2009

Wind is suddenly screaming into the cockpit of this aging
Antonov biplane. Charts and a half-assed, handwritten
flight plan whip by my face and through the cockpit door
into the main cabin. In the rear of the plane our director of
photography, Evan, who has been filming out the open door, is
suddenly thrust forward toward the edge of open space, only to
be yanked to a stop by his four-point harness. Documents eject
past him and into oblivion.

The sound is deafening and the pressure change so abrupt
that I try to brace my arm against the roof to steady myself.
Instead, my hand is forcefully bent back by what feels like
icicles slicing through my fingers, and I instinctively retract.

Open air. I'm immediately overwhelmed by a terrible
realization. *The cockpit ceiling is gone.*

Our audio engineer, Mike, has the common sense to kick
the pilot's door shut from his first-row seat behind me, closing
off the wind tunnel coursing through the interior of the plane
and sealing me into the roofless cockpit.

Moments ago I was actually bored, fiddling with a
camcorder to get a close-up of the plane's antiquated controls

----

and weathered gauges, the altimeter needle quivering from the vibration of the plane's beleaguered engine. The pilot, a stout Russian in a thick wool sweater, was languidly operating the stick. Now I'm craning back to get a view of the tail stabilizer through the gaping maw above me, praying the debris from the roof hasn't clipped it on the way by. I think twice about unbuckling my harness for a better look and instead concentrate on the ground below, which is getting closer by the second.

I probably shouldn't be surprised by any of this, of course. As the host of the Syfy Channel's *Destination Truth*, I've spent the last four years traveling to far-flung locales following reports of cryptozoological creatures and paranormal phenomena. Since there aren't exactly nonstop commercial flights leading directly to the doorsteps of the world's most enduring mysteries, I've made a career, such as it is, out of flying on board the planet's most laughably derelict aircraft.

But even by my admittedly lax standards, this plane is a piece of shit. I arrived at the airfield (and I do mean field) after two straight days of begging our field producer, Allison, to procure a plane—any plane—that could take us up and over the purportedly haunted Hoia Baciu Forest, the subject of our current episode. After exhausting every possible charter from here to Bucharest, she managed to find this flying Russian coffin and offered a few bucks to a local pilot to coax it back into active service.

The Antonov An-2 is not the sort of plane most people would agree to climb aboard in the first place. Basically unchanged since its design in 1946, it has wings covered in fabric, not metal. The plane is a flying dinosaur, originally intended for agricultural use. A function it might still fulfill as it threatens to fertilize nearby farms with the remains of my crew.

It is common in moments of potentially fatal catastrophe for the world to close in around us and become much smaller. Disaster is often countermanded by an intense focus, even if it happens to resolve on strange and seemingly arbitrary details. Looking over at the captain, I'm suddenly engrossed by his bald head. Where once there was a comical comb-over, there is now this emancipated ribbon of hair dancing in the vortex and joyfully reaching up to the heavens. It looks like one of those inflatable noodles outside a used-car dealership. Like any pilot worth his salt, though, he seems utterly unfazed by his new coif or by our circumstances in general. Where can one buy a little of that *Right Stuff* bravado required to shrug off the fact that your airplane is now a convertible?

When Captain Chesley Sullenberger famously ditched that crippled US Airways jet in the Hudson River after a flock of geese turned themselves into engine-flavored pâté, it barely seemed to raise his pulse. He casually noted to air traffic control, "We're gonna be in the Hudson," as though he was stopping off there for a cup of coffee. My distress call would have consisted of a jumbled litany of swearwords arranged in no particular order followed by an ecstatic, *"Holy JESUS we're going to crash into a river! MOMMY!"* During this particular aviation mishap, I do my best to stay calm and not soil my pants. This is the best I can muster under the circumstances, and I'm feeling fairly heroic about it.

The pilot adjusts the flaps and begins to bank around toward an open field. Time continues to slow down, and I think about the circumstances that brought me to this moment.

How did it come to this? How on earth did I end up here, plummeting in a partially disassembled biplane toward some anonymous field in Romania? A few years ago this would have been inconceivable. But now it's just another day at the office. I manage to catch the pilot's gaze for only a moment; above the din he leans over and yells, *"We must go back."*

Indeed. We must. Five years, to be exact.

2: 19,340

Above the arid plains of Tanzania's grasslands, the mighty
silhouette of Kilimanjaro rises like a dusty temple, a singular
cone breaking up the endless, supine earth. In the adjacent
town of Moshi, where locals beat back the sweat and heat
of 110 degrees, it seems inconceivable that the distant white
frosting on Kilimanjaro is actually glacial ice. But from up
here, it's a different world altogether.

At 11,000 feet, I squint in the chilly twilight to follow the
narrow trail beneath my feet. The landscape is utterly alien,
and a soupy mist clings to the rock face by my side. I run my
hand along the smooth stones for balance, my fingers red from
the icy water trickling down from above.

Just before sunset, my group and I finally stumble into
Shira Camp. The darkening haze is punctured by the welcome
sight of dozens of glowing orange tent domes. This is one of
several camps that temporarily cradle countless expeditions
ascending the side of Kilimanjaro. But our relief at arriving
here is short-lived. Rain suddenly buckets down, and porters
scramble to assist with tents as night arrives unceremoniously.
By the time I finally get into my own shelter, water is seeping

up through the seams in the floor; I'm shaking cold as I strip down, searching for drier clothes.

I came to Africa as something of a personal challenge. Almost exactly a year before this day, I looked in the mirror and decided to change who I saw looking back. I had been living in Los Angeles for more than five years, hustling to find work as an actor while slowly building a photography business on the side. But contrary to my naïve expectations, being a Hollywood actor/photographer did not automatically come hand in hand with a disposable income and the company of beautiful models. So, to support my ambitions and pay my rent, I was mostly waiting tables.

At Tufts University, I had double majored in drama and archaeology in what must have seemed like an attempt to force my parents into an early grave. Because if it's one thing America is clamoring for, it's guys who dig in the dirt with a flair for the dramatic. Luckily, my parents were empathetic. My mother, a vivacious and free-spirited young woman, grew up in tumultuous 1960s England and somehow found my father, a charming American deep-sea diver and self-made man. The two of them were endlessly supportive of my interests and passed on to me their humor and a confidence to follow my own path, as they had done.

But with no prospect for actually earning a dime as a young archaeologist, I tried my hand at acting, a passion since my breakout performance as "Bottom" in a high school production of A Midsummer Night's Dream. With Los Angeles casting directors somehow overlooking the rave reviews from my hometown newspaper, the Manchester Cricket, I was auditioning often but working little. I found myself jumping

at every opportunity I could to leave L.A. and escape into the
unknown. I had already driven across America seven times,
canvassing every state in the country, save one (I'm coming for
you, Oregon). I had been to Europe, the Caribbean, Mexico,
and Bangladesh, and spent several summers in Israel excavating
the ruins of the Roman city of Caesarea.

Travel, when undertaken habitually, becomes a potent
intoxicant. After all, who among us hasn't stared at perfume
ads, Corona commercials, and Thai Airways billboards
and been lost in a coconut-scented what-if? It is most often
detectable in a telltale faraway gaze observable on the faces of
married men vacationing in the tropics. They dream, if only for
a moment, of shedding their identity, abandoning their earthly
possessions, and opening a tiki-themed bar on the beach, toes
in the sand.

Travel is also Newtonian: it has a sort of momentum.
Unless interrupted by crying babies, work obligations, or an
empty bank account, it *wants* to remain in motion.

In my case, I didn't just keep moving. I accelerated.
As each trip came to an end, I grew discomposed in less
and less time, fidgeting to start another adventure. Within
weeks I started typing random destinations into online travel
sites, searching for cheap airfares and plotting out fictional
escapades. I got quick fixes with the occasional debauched
weekend in Vegas or a listless drive up the Pacific Coast
Highway. I was hooked. And suddenly my life as an actor took a
backseat to my dreams as a traveler.

Then I looked in the mirror. I felt older. I wasn't a kid in
school anymore. I was considerably overweight, bored, and
generally unhappy. I tried to combat this malaise by going to

the gym with some regularity. Without a specific goal, though, I slipped back into bad habits and comfortable routines.

Thinking back on it now, I can't remember what turned me on to the idea of climbing a mountain. Beyond the stairs to my apartment, I don't think I'd ever climbed anything in my life, let alone one of the famed Seven Summits. But once I settled on the idea, Kilimanjaro seemed a logical choice. Along with being suitably exotic, Kili is a non-technical climb that offered exactly what I was looking for: a goal that would challenge but (probably) not kill me. A sword of Damocles that would intimidate me into changing my lifestyle. I paid in full for the climb and, with a 365-day runway ahead of me, had all the motivation I needed. Every morning that I lay in bed thinking about not working out, I simply imagined my broken body frozen in mountain ice. I promptly got up and went to the gym.

To assist me in this venture, I assembled possibly the least qualified climbing team on the planet. My first recruit was my great friend Aron Epstein, because if there's one thing the Jews are known for, it's accomplishments in high-altitude mountaineering. Aron can't weigh more than one hundred pounds, and I'd go on record as estimating that at least a quarter of that comes from the bottles of hand sanitizer hidden in his jacket. Neurotic, brilliant, hilarious, and, most important, recently unemployed and independently wealthy enough to join this suicide run, he seemed a logical choice. The expedition was rounded out by Colin MacNaughton, a longtime friend, travel soul mate, and software engineer who smokes like a chimney and has a thing for high-end Scotch. Colin lives in San Francisco, where they have steep hills that I presumed he must have walked up occasionally, probably while smoking. This seemed like qualification enough at the time.

With my dream team in place, I got down to business. I trained throughout the year. Really went at it. I ran like a hamster in a wheel, took endless hikes in the Hollywood Hills, and endured no less than three different personal trainers. Grave adjustments to my diet followed (sayonara, fast food) and by year's end I had lost eighty pounds and was in the best shape of my life. The day after Christmas 2005, my compatriots and I boarded a flight to Africa, giddy at the prospect of adventure.

It takes about a week to ascend Kilimanjaro, with stops at various camps to acclimate to the extreme altitude. Each day becomes progressively harder as the thin mountain air provides less sustenance. We are climbing what is known as the Machame Route, or "Whiskey Route," so named because it is decidedly more serious than the standard Marangu Route, or "Coca-Cola Route."

Once the rain passes at Shira Camp, Aron, Colin, and I enjoy a terrible meal together and then crowd into a single tent to keep warm and engage in our nightly ritual of playing Scrabble. It is New Year's Eve. At ten minutes to midnight, we put down our wooden game tiles, throw on our down jackets, and shuffle out into the cold. Earlier in the evening we invited strangers from all over the camp to join us, and for the first few minutes it looks as if nobody is going to show. Then, tent by tent, lanterns come on, zippers unzip, and a group of hearty souls emerge to ring in the new year on the frigid side of a dormant volcano. Warm embraces erupt among German climbers, Japanese millionaires, and Tanzanian porters. An Australian woman has smuggled up a small bottle of champagne, which we all pass around and drink in shared communion near the roof of Africa.

I'm suddenly struck by the idea that people all over the world are gathering in places like this. Uncommon places. Unthought-of places. In my mind, New Year celebrations had always been the domain of city squares, crowded bars, and drunken house parties. I close my eyes and wander the world for a few moments to imagine a couple embracing on the deck of a sailboat in the Pacific, science crews popping champagne at the South Pole, submariners shaking hands at stations deep beneath dark waves, and nomads gathered by firelight in desert wadis. Something is shifting in me. *At this very moment.* My view is expanded somehow. I'm suddenly aware of an almost uncontrollable *need* to find these places, to be *with* these people. This is the moment that I become a traveler in earnest.

The next day our guide calls us aside and asks if we'd like to alter our route to a trail known as the Western Breach. This takes me by surprise, since we'd carefully chosen the Machame Route almost a year ago. It's unorthodox to make a change like this mid-climb, and it takes a few minutes of listening to his pitch while carefully studying a map to realize what he's proposing. The new route would be nearly two full days shorter and therefore financially beneficial to the porters, who could deposit us back to Moshi earlier and link in with their next group. We discuss the option, but it involves a much more direct ascent to a campsite perched inside the summit crater. Aron has already lost his appetite at this altitude, and climbing faster seems a dangerous gamble. We choose to stay on course. I don't know it at the time, but this decision may actually save our lives.

An expedition from our outfitter traveling along this more direct route will be caught in a rock slide cascading from the summit. When the dust settles, three American climbers will be dead. Several more will be seriously injured and airlifted to Nairobi. News of this won't reach my team until we return to Moshi. For now, the sight of a distant helicopter circling around the far side of the summit barely catches my attention.

Our last night is spent at Barafu Camp, perched at an uncomfortable 15,000 feet. All of us are feeling the effects of altitude at this point. I have a relentless headache pulsating through my temples. Aron, after being spoon-fed his dinner the night before, has mustered a recovery and is eating again. Colin, however, is on the decline. He has developed a deep cough that seems to worsen by the hour, and there are now a few broken capillaries on his face. Our nightly Scrabble game is played more out of obligation than enjoyment. We sit in a daze and attempt to place letters on the board. Our minds are doughy at this height, and our most impressive play is the word "dogs" for a measly six points. The game is abandoned, and we lie down in silence.

The final push to the summit of Kilimanjaro is particularly taxing. With almost no sleep, we rouse at eleven p.m. to gear up for the bid. At three miles above sea level, the temperature is well below freezing. We struggle into layer after layer of clothes, barely able to catch our breath. Our guide's inspirational pep talk consists of one very straightforward sentence: "Keep walking."

It is inky black. The narrow beam from my headlamp illuminates a dull blue-white circle of frozen earth two feet in front of me. With my hood pulled up and my goggles iced over, I can't see anything else. Occasionally an ankle will drift into the far edge of my light, my only indication that I'm following someone. We walk uphill for more than six hours. Within the first hour, the water hose on Colin's CamelBak freezes solid, and my beard becomes caked in ice. Every so often one of us will yell out, and we'll stop to pee or rest our legs. It's a long night of shared solitude; nobody has the strength to talk, and it's too late to turn back now.

As the first incandescent glow of morning arrives, we lower our hoods and remove our goggles. My knees have had it, Aron seems exhausted, and Colin looks like death frozen over. His face is an unrecognizable shade of gray, and he is now coughing blood. After a few false rises on the trail, we encounter the huge wall of glacial ice that rests atop Kilimanjaro's peak. In the far distance I spot a wooden sign and quietly begin to cry. I continue trudging forward, embarrassed that my teammates will see my tears, but I really can't contain myself. I've looked at pictures of that sign a thousand times in preparation for this moment. Though I'm still too far away to read it, I begin to recite it in my head:

CONGRATULATIONS!
YOU ARE NOW AT
UHURU PEAK, TANZANIA, 5895M. AMSL.
AFRICA'S HIGHEST POINT
WORLD'S HIGHEST FREE-STANDING MOUNTAIN
ONE OF WORLD'S LARGEST VOLCANOES
WELCOME

We take the last few steps together, touch the sign, and embrace. Emotions are now flowing freely, and we turn to look out at a vista that I'm far too poor a wordsmith to describe. The African Masai call it "Ngaje Ngai" or "The House of God." We'll just leave it at that.

As I look out over East Africa, past ice and down through grasslands, I am overcome by an electric sensation of accomplishment and joy. The thoughts that bubbled up in me a few nights before are now solidified. And though I don't yet know how, I promise to make travel my way of life. The answer, as it turns out, is waiting for me at the bottom of the mountain.

The hike down to Moshi normally takes a few days. We manage to do it in only one on account of the fact that I'm pretty sure Colin is about to die. We bypass the midway camp to get him close to a hospital in the event that his condition declines even further. (When traveling in rural Africa, it's important to not actually *go* to a hospital until the patient is on the brink of expiration, otherwise things are apt to get worse.)

Back at the hotel, we are stunned to learn about the deaths of the other climbers. We had met them, briefly. A shared cab ride into town to pick up last-minute supplies. I remember shaking their hands in a cramped jalopy. Now their surviving friends are crying uncontrollably. One man sits facedown on a stoop, cradling his bandaged head, and another, numb with grief, dials out on a satellite phone to tell his children that their mother is dead.

In the ensuing years, people have sometimes told me they've heard Kilimanjaro is "easy" to climb. What I took away from witnessing the broken climbers in Moshi was this: *Everything is easy until it isn't.* It's a philosophy that has served me well. Never underestimate any situation while traveling. At any moment, even a gentle slope can collapse. It's best to be ready for it.

The Internet connection is predictably pathetic at the sweltering cybercafé in town. My e-mail loads in spurts as an overhead fan with a missing blade circumscribes an awkward arc above me. Preliminary news reports about the rock slide carried the headline "Three American Climbers Die on Kilimanjaro," and my teammates and I have a lot of anxious e-mails to answer from friends and family. Among the many messages, I notice one from a producer in Los Angeles. It's marked "Urgent." I click to find a single sentence staring back at me:

"WHEREVER YOU ARE. COME HOME NOW."

3: Meet Neil Mandt

Hollywood, California, 2006

The author of the e-mail is a Hollywood television producer named Neil Mandt, who is, without a doubt, the most well-traveled person I've ever met. To know Neil is to have a strong opinion about him. He's a short-statured producer with a lot of irons in a lot of fires, even if half those fires are the result of arson. He's got a few Emmys, a very successful show on ESPN, a bachelor pad in the Hollywood Hills, and an expensive sports car. These are all facts of which Neil will happily remind you. At a cocktail party he once called me over to two Swedish lingerie models and demanded indignantly, "Tell these girls who I am."

I replied, "Ladies, this is Neil. He's kind of a prick." Neil didn't find this nearly as funny as the two girls did, but when underwear models are in play, all bets are off. Those are the rules, Neil. Those are the rules.

In a word, Neil is shameless. And I don't mean that in a bad way. Just the opposite. His brash, straight-shooter disposition makes him a true original, not to mention a deliciously embarrassing wild card in public. He'll talk to anyone at any time. No bones about it. As we were paying our check at a fancy steak house on Sunset Boulevard one night, he turned to me and whispered, "You see who that is?"

I gazed around the room, not focusing on anyone in particular.

"That's Sharon Stone," he exclaimed.

In fact, yes, it was Sharon Stone. In fairness, I should be forgiven for not recognizing her, since she was wearing a turban. An honest-to-God turban with a jewel right in the middle of it. She looked like Carnac the Magnificent.

"You want to go talk to her?" He grinned.

"No. NO. Neil, do not embarrass me in front of Sharon Stone. I'm begging you. Please."

Neil slipped out of the booth and sauntered right up to her table while I tried to blend in with the wallpaper behind him. "Excuse me," he barked.

I just about wilted as she looked up from her dinner. And then Neil said the single most improbable thing I've ever heard in my entire life. "I'm Neil Mandt," he said. "I directed you in that Turkish TV show."

"Wait, what?" I said.

Sharon Stone's eyes went wide under her turban, which made her look like an alien from *Mars Attacks!* "Oh my GOD! Neil! How have you been?!" she beamed.

And that's Neil Mandt for you. Just when you're ready to write him off, he turns out to be a secret Turkish television director who's on a first-name basis with Sharon Stone. The man's a complete mystery.

I first met Neil when I moved into his old place, a sweltering apartment with no air-conditioning on the twelfth floor of a Hollywood high-rise. I spent most of my five-year residency in my underwear attempting to avoid heat exhaustion as blistering sunshine baked in through the large bay windows. These windows looked directly onto the roof of Grauman's Chinese Theatre. Incidentally, on almost every postcard of Grauman's, you can see my bedroom window above the copper green roof. Sometimes I look closely at those cards and wonder if I was there when they were photographed (and whether I had any pants on at the time). Neil had relocated to another unit in the building, and we occasionally chatted in the halls. One day while we rode together in the elevator, Neil turned to me and said, "I just sold a competition reality show to ESPN. You'd be perfect for it." He asked me to turn in a two-minute audition tape.

The show was designed as a cross-country race where two teams would bullshit their way across America with no money and only the clothes on their backs. Along the way, the contestants would attempt to complete difficult sports-related challenges. Now, I'm not much for sports, but I *am* full of bullshit. Practically invented the stuff. This project seemed right up my alley. I immediately cleared my schedule of waiting tables at a steak house inside The Magic Castle, a private club for professional magicians (about which I could fill a three-volume exposé). Neil encouraged me not to simply sit in front of a camera and prattle on about why I'd be a good candidate for the show. "You need to make it interesting: talk your way into a place or fool somebody. That's what the show is going to be all about."

And so, a few days later, I got in my car with a friend and drove straight to Disneyland, famous for their ultratight security. Talking my way into the theme park seemed like a worthy challenge. My friend filmed me from afar as I marched up to the front gate. I told the security guard that my asthmatic brother and I had just exited the park and that he left his inhaler inside. When the guard informed me that he'd need to call a supervisor, I went for broke, adding that the little guy was in the throes of an asthma attack in the parking garage. There was no time to lose! The guard gave in, and within thirty seconds I was skipping down Main Street U.S.A. with a candy apple in my hand. I don't even have a brother. Forgive me, Walt. Those were desperate times.

The tape went to Neil and then to channel executives, and I quickly became a contestant on ESPN's inaugural reality show, *Beg, Borrow & Deal*. And beg, borrow, and deal I did. I sang the national anthem at a Major League Baseball game (sorry, Brewers fans, I was off-key). I caught a pass from an NFL quarterback (after more than a few fumbles in Giants Stadium) and even got a Boston Red Sox tattoo on the bottom of my foot (Go Sox). Over seventeen days, my team and I raced across a dozen states, eviscerated the competition, and won the show.

With this as preamble, I already knew that when Neil Mandt calls, interesting and immoral things often follow. But on this particular occasion, Neil's Bat-Signal found me far from home. I had just completed a yearlong gauntlet to the summit of Kilimanjaro and was about to reward myself by going on safari with my mates. My professional plans beyond that involved getting as drunk as possible on a beach in Zanzibar. Neil would have to wait.

I touched down in Los Angeles a few weeks later. Neil had since e-mailed frantically, demanding that I contact him as soon as I landed. I called from the baggage claim at LAX. He welcomed me home with a touching "Where the hell have you been?" and told me to come straight to his office. Do not pass go. Do not collect $200.

Neil's production company sits behind an anonymous door on Santa Monica Boulevard. The place is unnervingly dark and sprawling inside, giving visitors the feeling they might get mugged at any turn. Upstairs, Neil occupies a corner office that is completely overrun by cats. Written on the whiteboard behind his desk are titles of projects that Neil is working on, both real and never to be realized. Most of these projects are unlikely sounding at best. On this particular day, Neil is sitting in an oversized executive chair stroking a kitten, like Ernst Blofeld. The dry-erase board seems to have been wiped almost clean save for the title of a questionable home makeover show concocted by Neil. Written in thick blue marker are three words: "*Extreme African Village.*" I can't even bring myself to ask, and I silently pray that this isn't the project for which I've been summoned. I tip a chair forward, spilling out a couple of felines, and take a seat. I'm filthy. My beige safari shirt is streaked with dirt, and my red beard has been growing for over a month. I actually have one of those neck beards at this point, which makes me look like a grimy Civil War reenactor. "I've sold a show to SciFi that I want you to host," Neil says, flatly. (It will be a few years before the Channel becomes "Syfy," courtesy of a transformative rebranding that trades in two full-time vowels for two part-time vowels.)

"What's the concept?" I ask.

"It's about a guy who goes around the world hunting monsters." He smiles. I let that soak in for a few seconds. I proceed to point out that my résumé doesn't exactly read like Van Helsing's. Though I'm well traveled, to date I have little experience that would qualify me to work with monsters, other than serving overpriced steak to professional magicians.

"You're perfect," Neil explains. "They don't want a nut. They want a real traveler, a guy who isn't afraid to turn some rocks over. Someone funny."

I'm not taking any of this very seriously. You have to understand that almost every conversation about potential projects in Hollywood is a conversation about nothing. Industry people make a second career out of discussing things that are "in the works." There's an entire anthology of phrases like this that are utterly meaningless. People might tell you that they "have a few projects cooking" (eating at Quiznos later), some "exciting meetings coming up" (blood bank at one p.m.), or are "changing their representation" (moving back in with their parents). The idea that I've got a shot at being a modern-day TV Indiana Jones isn't something that I'm willing to consider with any amount of gravitas.

"So, what happens now?" I ask incredulously.

"Go to this address tomorrow at eleven a.m."

I reach over and take a Post-it note out of Neil's hand.

"Oh, and don't change your clothes. Don't even shower. Come just like this."

I begin to protest and Neil cuts me off. "*Just. Like. This.* Trust me."

I relent, surrendering to the idea and to another night in these filthy clothes. The whole thing feels like it's shaping up to be a disaster.

But hey, at least I'm not hosting *Extreme African Village*.

4: Underdressed for Success

Universal City, California, 2006

As I drive to the SciFi offices the next morning, there are a few key things I don't yet know. Most importantly, that Neil has already filmed a pilot presentation of this monster-hunting extravaganza. Though almost all of the footage from this deliciously awful pilot was disposed of in a top-secret NBC incinerator, I later learn that Neil himself acted as the host (naturally). The highlight of the piece was Neil's interview with a bewildered South American farmer, conducted while an assistant producer in a full Chupacabra costume performed a reenactment in an adjacent chicken coop. SciFi wisely deemed that the initial concept undergo a little retooling.

Since the show needs a new host, the Channel insists on conducting a proper casting call. Neil went to bat for me while I was summiting Kilimanjaro, and the best he could do was to convince them to meet me, alongside three other hosts hand-selected from the general casting. I am the long shot and don't even know it.

At this time, SciFi already has a huge reality hit on their hands with a show called *Ghost Hunters*. For those who aren't familiar, *Ghost Hunters* centers around two Roto-Rooter plumbers turned professional paranormal investigators. (And people say there's nothing original on television.) In the following years, the Channel will develop *Ghost Hunters International*, *Ghost Hunters Live*, and, most recently, *Ghost Hunters Academy*. (By the time this book goes to press, I'm sure they'll be airing *Dancing with the Ghost Hunters*, *So You Think You Can Ghost Hunt*, and *The Real Housewives of Ghost Hunters*.) But for now, in 2006, they're just looking for a sister act to this flagship paranormal program to kick off the 10:00 p.m. hour.

I arrive nearly a half hour before my meeting. After parking, I ascend to the main plaza, craning my head up at the looming Universal Tower. The building is a slate-colored rhomboid block that looks about as inviting as a steel coffin. It appears infinitely harder to climb than Kilimanjaro, and for the first time I'm starting to feel extremely nervous about all of this. In the austere lobby, I proceed to the security desk to check in. The guard looks up at me and furrows his brow. For a moment I'm unsure what to make of his expression, until I realize that he thinks I might be a vagrant. I've taken Neil's advice and not changed any of my clothes from the day before. I was so tired from the flight that I even fell asleep with my boots on. Now I'm stinking to high hell and looking like a train hobo. He glances down at my feet, no doubt wondering if I'm going to pee on the lobby floor. I fork over my ID and he prints out a pass for me, clearly surprised to find me in the computer system. "Fourteenth floor," he says warily.

The elevator opens, and I cautiously emerge into the SciFi offices. If I had any reservations about not showering and changing before, I now realize that I've made a full-blown mistake. The SciFi lobby is gleaming white, like a leftover set piece from *2001: A Space Odyssey*. You could do surgery in here, it's so clean. Across from the front desk, a series of flat-screen televisions play commercials for the Channel. Everyone who appears in these spots is suspiciously more attractive than I am.

The secretary who sits across from these screens is named Alex. This is a woman you do not want to mess with. An unflappable sentry, she probably wouldn't bat an eye if I walked up to her with a grenade in my hand. Over the next three years Alex will refuse to remember my name, even though I will be added to the roster of individuals continuously appearing on the monitors four feet from her face. Later, when executives joke about how I'm a "big star" on the Channel, I will raise a finger in protest. "When Alex learns my name, I've arrived at SciFi. Until then, I'm nobody."

Today we meet for the first time. She looks up from behind a plastic tub of fireball candies and unceremoniously hands me a clipboard to sign in. As I write my name, I notice three other signatures. I peek into the waiting area at my competition. Three other candidates, all of whom are wearing nice suits. I haven't had a chance to smell them yet, but I'm reasonably certain that they've showered, too.

The three guys regard me with a combination of amusement and pity. I pick up a copy of *Sci Fi* magazine and try to distract myself by delving into an in-depth profile piece on *MacGyver* star Richard Dean Anderson. I glance up to better take stock of the trio. Along with being well dressed, they all strike me as, well, a little like game-show hosts. I'm not exactly recovering my confidence, but I'm feeling marginally secure that these men do not represent the best and the brightest of American monster hunters. One by one, they are beckoned down the hall and out of this antiseptic space dock. They're each gone for what feels like an eternity, and by the time I hear my name called I know just about everything there is to know about Richard Dean Anderson.

"Josh. They're ready for you."

I'm led into an office at the far end of the hall. As I enter, I'm horrified by how many people are crammed into this room. All of them look up at me, and aside from Neil, none of them are smiling. Though it's impossible for me to determine everyone's title, there's no question as to who's running the show. Mark Stern, the senior vice president of the Channel, is the only person who looks comfortable in here, a sure sign that this is his domain. I reach out to shake his hand, and he invites me to sit down. Stern is one of those people who really *look* at you when you speak to him. It's as complimentary as it is unnerving—which is, I suspect, just how he likes it.

I'm getting a pretty good once-over from the whole group and feel compelled to break the ice. "Hi," I manage. "Let me . . . start by apologizing for my appearance. I just got off a plane from Tanzania." Smiles all around.

A perceptible sea change is underway. These people suddenly detect an authenticity to me. We talk for a few minutes; I recount my exploits on Kilimanjaro and discuss my interest in travel. I'm hoping that someone will bring up Richard Dean Anderson, but no such luck. I can't really tell how the interview is going, so I just do my best to come off appropriately adventurous. Stern's half smirk reveals that he can see right through my bullshit, but there's a warmth there too. Under less formal circumstances I suspect we'd get along great. I also have a few nice exchanges with Rob Swartz, the affable development executive in charge of the project. At this point the only thing I know for sure is that these people no longer consider my dirty beard and tattered shirt the potential markings of a deranged serial killer.

After it's all over, I shake hands with the network brass and walk out of the office. Neil sees me to the elevator and tells me that I did well. I step inside and put my hand up to hold the closing doors. "What's this pilot called, anyway?"

"*Destination Truth*. Now go take a shower," he says. "You stink."

Adventures in
Monster Hunting and
Professional Ghostology

5: "We Found Something!"

Kuala Lumpur, Malaysia, 2006

After my meeting with the Channel, things progress quickly. A call comes in a few days later with good news: I got the job. The Channel has ordered a second pilot, and I'm told that if things go well, I could end up with a series. Rather than reshoot the original pilot in South America, a decision is made to film in Southeast Asia, where recent sightings of a Bigfoot-like creature in the jungles of Malaysia have made headline news. For my part, I mostly nod and let plans unfold, all but certain that this entire enterprise will collapse long before I actually board a plane.

A crew is cobbled together, mostly comprising people already working for Neil's company. Neil shuffles our itinerary no less than six times, and then, a few days before we're set to depart, the crew convenes at my new apartment in Silver Lake to film the opening scenes of the show. I meet Eric, Neil's hardworking and earnest young producer, who is clearly doing most of the heavy lifting while garnering none of the credit. Blake, our exhausted-looking tech manager, arrives, as does Marc Carter, Neil's longtime friend and an experienced director of photography. Carter has a devil-may-care disposition and seems perpetually bemused by Neil. I suspect that he's going to be a good ally on the road. The group is rounded out by Nick Scown, an editor-cum-field producer, who doesn't seem particularly confident about any of this, which probably means that he's the smartest guy in the room.

Once this motley crew assembles, Neil loosely directs a sequence where we pack gear and discuss the recent Malaysian sightings. All of this is being filmed in my living room, remember. I kick a stack of dirty laundry aside, Frisbee a Domino's pizza box into the kitchen, and tack a world map on my wall in a desperate attempt to transform my tiny bungalow into Team Truth headquarters. MI-6 it is not, but there is an authenticity, I suppose; I do live here, after all. Before we start filming, I ask Neil what to wear on the show, whereupon he promptly rifles through my closet. He picks out a motorcycle jacket and jeans. It will not be until much later, in the heart of Malaysia, that I realize thick leather and denim are not sensible jungle attire. The living room shoot feels like something between an impromptu home movie and a student film, and I'm not confident that we're actually going to make it out of Los Angeles, let alone the country. Surely, someone will intervene and put a stop to all of this, right?

Wrong.

Hours later I'm sitting in the dim cabin of a Singapore Airlines jumbo jet somewhere over the endless black Pacific. Even though the aircraft's tracking map on the seat back in front of me indicates that we're en route to Singapore, I'm still in a state of giddy denial as I gaze at the blanket of stars outside my window.

Odd as it might seem, night on board a 747 is one of my

absolute favorite places on, or above, earth. I feel blissfully adrift up here and always have. When I was a child, my parents and I frequently flew to England to visit my grandparents. During the flight, my mother would lower our three tray tables and cover them with a blanket while I slipped down onto the floor of a makeshift cave. Enveloped by the darkness of 30,000 feet and cradled by the hum of those four massive Rolls-Royce engines, I would snuggle up and happily fall asleep.

Even as an adult, I'm struck by an implicit liberty to air travel that's often overlooked on account of cramped quarters. In actuality, we aren't constrained at all: we've broken free. In flight, we slip the heavy tether of responsibility and no longer belong to the world below. We are answerable to no one. Phones cease to ring, and our distractions are few. Even Time, that constant companion, loosens his grip around us. Entire days can be wound back or skipped over at these lofty heights, as we exist merely in a world of vapor. Adventures are both beginning and coming to a close up here as people from opposite ends of experience paradoxically move in one direction.

By now most of the plane's passengers are asleep, so I'm surprised to see Neil stumbling past my seat toward the forward lavatory. Neil is what you might call a sleeping pill enthusiast. He usually pops a Xanax with a glass of full-bodied Cabernet on short flights, or an Ambien CR, which is, as he likes to say, "the Mercedes-Benz of sleeping pills." However, on tonight's long-haul trip he's forgone his usual capsule cocktail for a double dose of a stronger pill that should come with a printed suggestion that users wear a diaper lest they soil themselves in a drug-induced stupor. The pill also prompts sleepwalking, a side effect that Neil is experiencing in full force as he marches down the aisle wearing nothing but boxer shorts. Though the plane is flying smoothly, Neil careens like a drunk in turbulence and manages to get himself into the bathroom, where he'll probably fall back asleep.

With the cabin now still, I quietly unbuckle my seat belt to take a stroll, a customary habit of mine on overnight flights. I tiptoe past the center staircase in my socks and then down the aisle of the main cabin. I happen upon a flight attendant in one of the galleys who could easily double as a supermodel (those who have flown on Singapore know that their hiring policies haven't evolved much since the 1960s). Recognizing that I can't sleep, she pours me a glass of red wine, and I curl up in the jump seat next to the emergency exit. We talk for a while, sharing broken conversation and laughing quietly in the otherwise silent cabin. She asks me why I'm headed to Southeast Asia. "I'm not entirely sure," I reply. "I'm looking for something."

She flashes a confused smile.

In the morning, my crew and I touch down in Singapore's eponymous capital city. The country is only 750 square miles, which makes it roughly half the size of Rhode Island. Its legendary reputation as a lawless pirate den stands in stark contrast to the strict modern government, sprawling air-conditioned mega malls, and gleaming skyscrapers. Orchard Road, once home to nutmeg and pepper plantations, is now lorded over by white-walled spas, expensive boutiques, and chic eateries. The sterility of present-day Singapore and its draconian legal system have made it something of a letdown to many an adventure traveler. (I myself am not a huge fan of any place that threatens to arrest and beat the shit out of me for spitting gum on the ground.) Still, if you're in the market for a Gucci handbag or a pair of Jimmy Choo stilettos, it's just the spot.

NBC (parent of SciFi) has mandated that we be accompanied, due to recent political upheaval in parts of the country. We exit the terminal and meet with our local security consultant, who will guide us across the border of Malaysia to Johor Bahru, the city nearest to the recent sightings. Subsequent experience has taught me that these security consultants come in only two varieties: trained killers and trained monkeys. Half the time, they are indispensable assets who speak regional dialects, navigate complex local customs, and offer practical advice for staying out of trouble. The other half of the time they turn out to be armed goons who are just as apt to accidentally shoot the clients as they are to protect them. In this particular case, we're saddled with a guy named Captain Gupta, and he's exhibiting early signs that we may not be in the hands of Southeast Asia's finest. I look on in disbelief as he gets lost trying to guide our jeep out of the airport. Despite it being a twenty-minute drive, he manages to take three wrong turns on the way to the Malaysian border and even stops to ask for directions at a local prison. I've never felt safer.

We cross the border with little fanfare, arriving in the city of Johor Bahru. This is one of the fastest-growing urban centers in Malaysia but maintains a slightly gritty disposition. The whole downtown could use a fresh coat of paint, and the presence of large manufacturing plants has done little to encourage tourism. Still, it feels entirely more authentic than the pristine metropolis of nearby Singapore.

We check into a hotel that looks like it's been shelled by artillery fire and meet in Neil's room to begin our operation in earnest. Bags are unzipped, and equipment spills out like entrails across the open floor. I attach a microphone to my shirt and slip the transmitter in my back pocket, fingering the power switch. We've been in motion for days, spanned the planet at half the speed of sound, driven across an international border, all to arrive at this moment, heralded by a tiny gesture that nobody else in the room observes. As the device clicks on, I sense that the microphone is now alive and waiting patiently for me to feed it. My previous fear that the project would never materialize is now replaced by much more solemn anxiety. It's happening. Right now. A hundred lightbulbs come on at once. I now see this pilot for what it really is: a completely unscripted television show where two cameras record my every move as I lead a team into the jungle looking for a potentially dangerous animal. I look down at the microphone and swallow hard. Here we go.

Since we don't really have a plan, we agree to drive north to Endau Rompin National Park, the epicenter of the sightings. That seems logical enough. There's just one problem: we don't have permission to film or even enter the park. In point of fact, we've been advised in a letter from Mr. Chu, a park representative, that we expressly *don't* have permission. Knowing that Mr. Chu works near the entrance to Endau Rompin, and with hopes of persuading him in person, we climb into two beat-up old SUVs and leave Johor Bahru in the dust.

By late afternoon the urban sprawl has receded and broad swaths of green jungle envelop the edges of the road. The air is sticky and hot as we pull over to the village at the perimeter of the national park. We make inquiries about Mr. Chu's whereabouts at the park office and discover that he's working at a camp deep in the jungle. Outside, I take a rag to my neck, and Neil and I squint over an old park map unfolded across the hood of our car. We exchange knowing glances and smile. Neil saunters back into the office. I call Eric over. "We need to head into the village and pick up some food for tonight."

"Why? I thought Chu wasn't here?" he says.

"He's not. We're going into the park to find him."

Eric stammers and then follows Carter and me into the village to look for a store. This is the hinterland, and the one outpost we do find has very little by way of food offerings, unless you consider quail eggs and rotting dragon fruit a hearty dinner. I bat away a swarm of black flies and slap a loaf of stale bread and a case of warm beer onto the counter. Carter throws down a box of cookies, and Eric grabs a tin of crackers. It isn't much, but it will have to do. Back at the park office we offload our gear into a proper 4x4. A Samoan-looking ranger fires up the engine.

The road is an absolute disaster. Deep ruts and thick mud cause the jeep to buck and slip as we head into the interior. A wooden bridge moans under our weight, and I look in the side mirror as a board behind us tumbles into the gorge. The sun is low in the sky when we finally arrive. The camp turns out to be some sort of research station perched beside a broad river. A few thatched huts shelter wooden tables, microscopes, and piles of papers. It looks abandoned; I can't help but feel as though I've just wandered into a set from *Tarzan*. Mr. Chu comes scampering across a rope bridge above the water. I can tell that it's him, since he's yelling at us in Malay and waving angrily at the cameras.

"You no have permission to be here!"

Well, this is off to a fine start. After we lower the cameras and let him cool off a little, he relents and allows us to remain.

This is lucky for us, since sunset is fast approaching, and we're low on options for accommodation. The best Chu can offer are three unoccupied cabins overlooking the camp. Content with the knowledge that we have someplace to lay our heads, we happily peel off our sweat-soaked clothes to swim in the river and clean up before dark. The heat is like a blanket, and as we dry off quickly on the bank, a five-foot snake descends through the canopy above me and slithers along the ground and into the water. This will be my last swim.

Twilight incites a nearly deafening hum of insects as the jungle comes alive. Mosquitoes begin biting my neck and moths punch me in the face as I head to one of the cabins. "Cabin" might be a generous term, actually. The buildings are actually seven-foot-by-seven-foot plywood shacks with nothing in them but a wooden platform elevated about four feet off the floor. It's right around this time that I hear Neil screaming. He peels out of his room and through his open door I can see a spider the size of a dinner plate clinging to the wall. My mouth falls open as I go in for a closer look. It's a huntsman spider with a leg span of nearly a foot, although from where I'm standing it looks suspiciously like the Face Hugger from *Alien*. Neil is nearly inconsolable and pleads with Mr. Chu for better accommodations. There are none to be had. To make matters worse, Gupta, our appointed security guard, has fallen asleep against a tree. With the realization that the rest of us aren't going to bed anytime soon, we set to work for the night.

Our plan is to interview eyewitnesses in nearby villages and then canvass as much of the surrounding jungle as possible, scanning for physical evidence. To aid in this effort, we're packing a night-vision scope, infrared cameras that help us to see in the dark, and a thermal imager used to detect natural radiation and thereby illuminate living things. This last gizmo is especially handy, since tigers and other predators are known to lurk in Malaysia's interior.

Chu directs us to a neighboring aboriginal village, and we steer the 4x4 along primitive access roads deep into the jungle. We arrive at a modest collection of houses at around eight p.m.; it's pitch-black here, and we exit the vehicle to the dim view of a few dozen people sitting around quietly in the dark. Dogs are barking loudly, and babies are crying somewhere close by. There are no less than six people in this village who claim to have seen Bigfoot personally, or so I'm being told by Gupta, who we've kicked awake to come along and translate. We're led into a small hut where a man tells me that he didn't actually see Bigfoot but believes he spotted a nest. He describes it at length, noting a foul smell in the area. We pinpoint the nearby region on a map and move to the next witness. I'm led into a barren two-room house made of hastily poured concrete. An old man sits on an empty floor with a single candle in front of him. I sit down, and we talk for a while in the flickering darkness. Behind him, I can barely make out his wife leaning motionless against the back wall, flies buzzing around her head. The man speaks to my translator in Malay for a few minutes, and I look up from the candle flame when I distinctly hear the word "orangutan."

"It looked like an orangutan?" I ask. "Is that what he's saying?"

"No. He says it *was* an orangutan."

This is intriguing, since these great apes, while native to Malaysia and Indonesia, are now found exclusively on the adjacent islands of Borneo and Sumatra. Fossil remains have been recovered on the Malaysian peninsula, however. Is it possible that a population of orangutans could have survived here in Malaysia's interior? It seems unlikely, but I'm suddenly energized that this man, as well as several others that I speak to, appear to have had some sort of a *legitimate* experience. I'm quickly realizing that we aren't just here looking for Bigfoot; we're here to document a mystery. There may be no Bigfoot. There may be no orangutans, for that matter. But there is clearly *something*, and I, for one, am increasingly engaged in the search.

We drive toward the sightings area along a logging road, and I let the cool night air wash over my face. Staring out into the black jungles, I run through the eyewitness testimony in my head and consider the possibility that somewhere in all of this dense rain forest a monster could be lurking. We park and then radiate out on foot into the jungle, powering up our cameras to give us some advantage in the darkness. We hike for a mile or more, looking for droppings, prints, the described nests, or any other physical remains. More than anything, we're just hoping to avoid getting bit by any of the peninsula's venomous snakes or spiders. We search for hours upon hours, eventually stopping to drink a little water and change tapes in the cameras. Eric points at Neil with his flashlight beam. "Neil. What's on your shirt?"

We all look over, and in the light we see a golf-ball-size bloodstain on the front of Neil's safari shirt. Neil lifts up the fabric to reveal a small puncture wound leaking blood down his stomach.

"Land leeches," Gupta says solemnly.

And with that little announcement, Neil rips off every

single piece of clothing he has on. Everything. He's suddenly naked and completely losing his shit. Even though the leech had already fallen off of him, there may be others, and he's not taking any chances.

In his defense, however, Malaysian leeches are truly horrifying creatures. They basically look like little brown worms but move like possessed Slinkys along the soggy ground. They are experts at sniffing out blood and sweat: the minute your foot hits the ground, you're fair game for an attack. Without your even noticing their presence, these leeches will rush your shoes, climb up under your pant legs, and sink their teeth into whatever part of your body they deem most delicious. As they bite, they inject an anticoagulant into the wound, which makes you bleed copiously until the leech gets its fill and drops off. We unenthusiastically check naked Neil over for additional parasites and, finding none, encourage him to put his clothes back on immediately.

Back at camp, Neil is still bleeding, and the spider is still clinging to the wall of his cabin. Fed up, he abruptly storms over to the 4x4, slams the door, and rolls up the windows. Eric joins him, and the two of them lock the car. The rest of us just stand there looking at each other. I walk over and knock gently on the jeep window, which Neil rolls down an inch.

"Hi there. And what in the hell are the rest of us supposed to do?"

"I don't know," Neil says sharply. "But I'm not getting out of this goddamned car."

Carter and I tentatively push open the door to our cabin. On the far wall is a tarantula the size of my hand. It skitters into the corner as we enter. Exhausted and out of options,

Carter and I lie down side by side on the wooden shelf. I make
the mistake of rolling over and peeking under the platform,
where I come eye to eyes with two additional spiders of an
unidentifiable but equally colossal variety clinging to the
underside. Carter and I keep all of our clothes and shoes on as
a layer of protection and slip a single mosquito net over both
of our heads. I tuck my exposed hands into my armpits, and
we unabashedly spoon each other for dear life. I'm not sure if
it's owing to fear or fatigue, but we somehow manage to forget
to film any of this; a pity, since, in the four seasons to follow,
the shacks in Endau Rompin remain the single worst sleeping
arrangement in *Destination Truth* history.

Morning finds me sore and cramped, but at least a giant
spider isn't stuck to my face. Carter and I make our way down
to the river, where we wash up in the cool water and eat rice
prepared by a local woman from the camp. I crack open a
warm beer as Neil and Eric come limping out of the car. At
least they didn't sleep any more comfortably than we did. After
packing up, we bid adieu to Mr. Chu and make the long drive
back toward Johor Bahru.

Back on the main road, we make a scheduled stop to
interview a man named Vincent Chow, a naturalist who works
with the government and seems to be the local authority on
Bigfoot. I'm half expecting him to be a loon, but instead he
turns out to be a fascinating and passionate scientist. He's a
gracious host, warmly welcoming us into his home, where we
talk for well over an hour. We sit barefoot in his study drinking
tea and discussing the endless variety of species in the jungles
of Malaysia. At one point in the interview, he leans in and
whispers, "Go into the jungle with curiosity, and you will find

beautiful things." A smile breaks out on his face. "The true secret to seeking the unknown is in the *looking*, not the *finding*. The journey is what matters."

I don't fully process it at the time, but he's just unwittingly homed in on the heart and soul of what *Destination Truth* will aspire to showcase.

With Vincent's words still ringing in my head, we drive back toward Johor Bahru. On the edge of the city, traffic suddenly comes to a grinding halt. Ahead of us, mobs of locals stream through the streets toward the lights of a passing parade. Carter grabs the camera, and we jump out of the jeep. Gupta, uncharacteristically concerned for my safety, quickly parks the car and comes running after.

The celebration turns out to be in honor of Chinese New Year, and we slip in between dancers, dragon puppets, and white-powdered dancers who wink at me from atop neon-lit floats. The streets are hot, humid, and utterly alive. I hop on the back of a truck full of Malaysian children and join the procession. Gupta scans the crowds as we go, trying to keep pace from the sidewalk. Carter bobs and weaves with the camera, documenting the frenetic crowd.

The night ends at a strange little bar down by the docks. We throw back more than a few drinks and reminisce about our misadventure into the jungle. I spin around on my stool to catch sight of one of the most beautiful women I've ever laid eyes on. She's alone at a corner table. I may be in love. Gupta sidles up beside me at the bar and leans into my ear. "Josh. That's a man."

My introduction into the pervasive "ladyboy" culture is a harsh one. Incidentally, here's a bit of rock-solid travel advice:

when getting hammered in a bar in Southeast Asia, make sure to kick the tires a little before you drive off the lot. As we spill out of the bar, I'm still in disbelief about the transvestite, but at least Gupta has finally earned his paycheck. Back at the hotel I head to my room and collapse. I smell like Chinese incense and American cigarettes and drift off to fitful dreams about spiders and cross-dressers.

The next morning we decide to enlist the help of a few local investigative groups that have a head start on researching the recent Bigfoot sightings. Eric has called and arranged for them to meet us at our hotel. I emerge from the elevator bleary-eyed and take in our eclectic recruits. Perched on a couch are three very attractive young women dressed all in black. They sit silently alongside an older man named "Uncle" who sports a mesh tank top and bright camo pants. Together the four of them make up a paranormal group called The Seekers and boast a Malaysian television show by the same name. Uncle jumps up and comes at me fast, vigorously shaking my hand and excitedly launching into news of another recent Bigfoot sighting. His authority is mitigated slightly by the fact that I can see his nipples. The Seekers girls don't appear to speak English and seem a little glazed over. As best I can tell, the premise of *The Seekers* show is that Uncle cavorts around in the dark with three submissive Malaysian girls twenty years his junior, looking for ghosts. I have no idea how he pulled off this arrangement, but the man is clearly a genius. Despite the sideshow quality of their group, Uncle has great local connections and will be a huge asset with logistics.

Nearby, a rather serious-looking collection of people mill about the front door. They're clearly identifiable as a group since they're all sporting matching shirts that read "SPI." "SPI" stands for "Singapore Paranormal Investigators," and while they may lack some of The Seekers' presentational flash, they seem infinitely more scientific. Rounding out this circus is Jan McGirk, a Californian reporter writing for the UK newspaper the *Independent*. This haphazard consortium is starting to feel like the cast of a Michael Crichton novel, and I'm hoping to get through the afternoon without being party to an act of international espionage or a dinosaur rampage.

After exchanging hellos and comparing notes, we all pile into our respective cars and motor out of Johor Bahru in convoy. Our destination is the rain forest of Kota Tinggi, a few hours from the city. Here, several large footprints were recently discovered and have been attributed to Bigfoot by the local press. A few hours of driving and we arrive on the outskirts of Kota Tinggi, where we park our cars just beyond a haphazard cluster of tin shacks and lean-tos. As we open our doors, a troop of monkeys scampers into the dense foliage along the side of the road.

Our first priority is to examine prints that were reported upriver, and for this we need a boat. A ragged collection of skiffs sits along a half-submerged dock, and we begin a lengthy haggling session with a few local fishermen. The Seekers girls, Uncle, and the SPI gang prove useless at negotiation, even though they're the ones who speak the language. We manage to talk the fisherman down from an astronomical starting price to something more appropriate, considering half of the boats are missing engines and most are visibly sinking. It takes another half hour of mechanical repairs before any of the motors will turn over. We bide our time in the shade, keeping a close eye on a young boy smoking a cigarette three inches from an open container of fuel. The last thing I need is for this kid to blow up the dock and take the entire Southeast Asian paranormal community with him.

Still waiting, I wander aimlessly along the road looking for the monkeys and spy a concrete structure obscured by clinging vines. I take one step into the jungle for a better look and am immediately surrounded by another world. The sound of banging wrenches and coughing engines has been replaced by the muffled sibilation of rain forest. Insects buzz, birds chirp, and with the sun diffused I feel eerily alone under the shady canopy. Upon closer inspection, the cement structure reveals itself to be a pillbox from World War II. These British-built bunkers are scattered all along the river and are part of what was once the Kota Tinggi defense line. Brigades were stationed in these remote bunkers to detect and beat back a potential Japanese assault. I crawl over the bunker and drop down to the narrow entrance in the back. The interior is badly flooded and crumbling, and I catch sight of a thick green snake slithering into the dark water. Based on my one eventful night in Endau Rompin Park, I can only imagine the forgotten exploits of soldiers stationed in this wilderness for months. However, stories in remote jungles like this are consumed like the bunker itself and eventually become hidden from the light forever. The whine of a running boat engine penetrates the forest, and I turn away from my imaginings and back to the road.

With the boat finally up and running, we speed upstream, cutting the glassy surface of the broad river like a blade. I lie down along the bow of the boat, pull a hat down over my face, and drift off to sleep in the breeze. I sit up when

I hear the motor idle down and see that we're edging up along the bank of the river. Jumping out onto the shore, we trek up into the jungle, which is every bit as thick and lush as Endau Rompin. We machete up a trail and emerge into a sandy clearing. "This is the place that footprints were found," the translator whispers nervously.

We divide up, scouring the soil for any signs of tracks, droppings, or other evidence that a large primate has been in the area. Nothing. The search goes on for hours, and late in the day we're advised to return to the boats, since tigers are known to inhabit the area. The guides cannot guarantee our safety after dark. As we push off the banks, rain arrives in sheets, dumping down on us. We spend the boat ride home ripping leeches off our legs and watching rivulets of blood trickle down the fiberglass hull of the boat.

Back at the dock, we find that the monkeys have shit on our car. More accurately, it appears as though they've shit on the car and then thoroughly rubbed it over every square inch of the entire vehicle like some sort of fecal hand wax. It's almost impressive in its disgustingness. Neil grumbles and swears, his relationship with Malaysia's animal kingdom already tenuous at best. Sensing that we're eventually going to get caught in the spider-infested darkness, he bows out of the final leg of the day to head back to Johor Bahru and begin his own investigation for the elusive filet mignon.

Back in the cars, we make our last stop at a swath of jungle to the north where additional prints were recently claimed. The convoy stops along a seemingly anonymous section of road. As I climb out of the vehicle, I hold up a newspaper photograph in front of me, dropping it down to reveal that I'm standing at the exact spot where it was taken. We're led into the jungle by our guides and scout around for prints. The search takes hours, and the day eventually grows long; the relentless humidity is exhausting. As we finally double back toward the road, I throw a few last glances along the ground and happen to notice a distinct marking in the nearby mud. I do a double take, see what appear to be toe prints, and quickly swat through the brush to get a better look. I call over the reporter, who happens to be standing closest to me. We both crouch down in disbelief at what is now unmistakably a footprint-shaped cavity. "Carter!" I scream out. "Get a camera over here!"

Before I know it, I'm surrounded by people staring down at a seventeen-inch-long mystery print. We scour for more, but the patch of mud is surrounded by hard earth and a few indistinct depressions. A Seekers girl pipes up and says, "Now what?" Good question. It never occurred to me that anything like this would actually happen, so I'm at an absolute loss as to what to do next. With cameras rolling, people crowding around me (and my career as a televised explorer possibly hanging in the balance), I'm hoping for a miracle. My salvation appears in the form of a slight-statured Singaporean girl from SPI who quietly says, "Should we cast it?"

I crane up from the dirt. "Hold on. Do you have casting powder?"

"Yes," she says enthusiastically, adding, "but I'm not really sure how to use it."

She hands me a box of powder marked "State Crime Lab." Even though I don't have a clue how to use this stuff, it's starting to get dark here in tiger town, and nobody else is taking the reins. I'm not all that keen on being eaten alive, and I'm pretty sure I've seen enough episodes of *CSI* to pull this off. I make quick work of mixing the powder with bottled water, and once the mix reaches the consistency of pancake batter, I start filling in the depression. It seems as though it's going to take some time to harden, so I quickly wash off my hands and grab the satellite phone out of Eric's bag.

I rush out to the middle of the empty road looking for a signal. I breathlessly punch in Neil's cell phone number and listen impatiently as the other end rings. "Hello?"

"Neil. It's Josh. We found something!"

I explain the situation, and I can hear him grabbing car keys and running out of his hotel room. There are a lot of considerations to be made, and both of us are talking them through as we think of them. At the forefront of our minds is the problem of dominion. For foreigners in Malaysia, it isn't easy to just stroll off with a Bigfoot print, especially considering the current media attention this story is getting. Neither of us wants to lose control of our find, but with a reporter, two other teams of investigators, and Malaysian nationals all over the scene, it's all but guaranteed that we're leaving these jungles empty-handed. We agree to at least photograph the casting extensively and make a duplicate print, if possible.

After hanging up, I return to the woods, where the plaster is now as hard as rock. Flicking open a Spyderco knife, I set to work on digging the impression out of the earth, working around the digits and loosening the surrounding dirt. By flashlight I extract the print, hoping not to break it in half in front of an audience. To my amazement the footprint pops out of the earth in one piece, and we quickly but carefully carry it out to the road. Uncle suggests that he bring the print to The Seekers' headquarters in

the capital city of Kuala Lumpur, where we can all reconvene
the next day. The sudden ownership exerted over the casting
doesn't come as a surprise. I manage to carve my name and the
date into the back of the plaster for posterity, and we photograph
the print from every angle.

The cast is wrapped rather unceremoniously in T-shirts
and loaded into the back of Uncle's truck. We head out and
eventually meet Neil at the intersection of the main highway.
He's absolutely beaming at the discovery. We all are. It's surreal.
We head back to our hotel in high spirits, stopping to eat
questionable but delicious chicken burgers from a street vendor
outside a gas station. I sit on the curb and devour the food with
a huge smile. Somewhere, a footprint with my name on it is
speeding through the darkness toward Kuala Lumpur.

In the morning we check out of our hotel, and I choke
on my coffee at the front desk when I notice a picture of me
on the front page of the Malaysian *New Straits Times*. Similar
pictures and accompanying articles appear in every newspaper
in the city. We're overnight celebrities in Malaysia. I snatch a
copy of each paper at a newsstand and have Gupta translate
them in the car as we head to Uncle's house. They're all very
complimentary and highlight that this find is going to be a
boon for the country's tourism sector. We're delighted to learn
that we're repeatedly referred to as "the American Expedition."

Exploding up through the canopy of the verdant jungles,
Kuala Lumpur, or KL as it's universally called, is nothing short
of an architectural mirage. No other metropolis on earth even
comes close to managing such an intense marriage between
untamed nature and modernity. Originally a malaria-infested
mining town, the city has punched up through the rain forest

to become one of the shining beacons of Southeast Asia. The shimmering tent poles of this unlikely metropolis are the mighty twin Petronas Towers. Like an *Arabian Nights* tale dreamed by a futuristic Scheherazade, the gleaming steel of these star-shaped spires rises to a dizzying 1,500 feet. Though they've now been eclipsed as the tallest buildings in the world, they are still arguably the most beautiful skyscrapers ever constructed. Beneath them, Malay, Chinese, and Indian cultures blend in a complex but seemingly balanced cultural soup that has been simmering for more than ten thousand years. One can hear the Islamic call to prayer from a Chinese market while the smell of Indian curry hangs in the air; a trip through KL is simply a joyous and confusing cultural mash-up.

Uncle's house lies in the suburbs of the city, and as we arrive I can't help but notice that there are a lot of cars in his driveway. I also can't help but notice that every single second- and third-floor window of the house is blocked entirely by sandals. Thousands of flip-flops press against the glass, giving the very real appearance that the whole house might actually explode and release a tidal wave of footwear across the city.

Inside, I'm amazed to see at least twenty reporters with cameras, microphones, and portable lights. The Seekers girls are milling about in their trademark black ensembles, which I'm starting to wonder if they sleep in. Uncle, on the other hand, has changed into a leopard-print velour top, which I guess is his press conference attire. He offers me a bowl of hot mutton soup, just what I need in this 105-degree heat. I see a staircase leading to the upper floors with loose sandals along the steps. "Uncle, I don't mean to pry, but what's the deal with the sandals?"

"I made a bad investment," he says. "It's a long story."

"I see."

"You're not a size nine, are you?" he asks hopefully.

"No. I'm afraid not."

On the back porch, the footprint has been moved into a glass display case (nice touch) and Uncle, who I'm quickly realizing is the P. T. Barnum of Southeast Asia, drifts off to glad-hand the press and milk this auspicious occasion for all it's worth. I'm stunned by the turnout, and Uncle and I take a seat in front of the press in his backyard to answer questions. I'm asked repeatedly if I think the print is legitimate evidence of Bigfoot. The short answer is that I have no earthly idea. Frankly, the print looks a little troubling to me. It's ungainly and doesn't appear overly anatomical. On the other hand, it was discovered in an anonymous corner of a vast forest, and I certainly can't account for how it got there. I tell the media my honest opinion: the print raises important questions and invites us all to continue the search. "This is a starting point, not an answer."

I look over at Neil, who nods slightly, approving of my monster-hunter diplomacy. A government representative has called during the press conference to confirm our suspicion that the print is the property of the government and must remain in Malaysia. Luckily, we're allowed to duplicate the cast. Using a plastic tub from a local hardware store, we lower the print into the mix and create a negative impression of the original. With the press looking on, I'm once again hoping not to crack this thing in half. Luckily, the duplication goes off without a hitch, and we head back into the city with a twenty-pound container of plaster in the backseat of our car.

We check into a posh hotel in the middle of downtown
KL and, to the horror of the staff, drag the massive tub through
the lobby. My arms and shirt are caked in white plaster, and I
ask the bellhop to please find a hacksaw and send it up to my
room. After a few hours using the hotel hair dryer, cutlery from
room service, and the saw, we extract the plaster, ruining the
rug and two butter knives in the name of discovery. The next
morning Neil sends most of the crew to the airport with the
print and all of our shot tapes. Everything is to be flown out
of the country and into the States as soon as possible. Even
though the government seems content with the original print,
our photos are now appearing in every paper in the city, and
we're erring on the side of caution.

The team departs, while Neil, Carter, and I stay behind
for some much-needed downtime. We hop the first flight to
Thailand for a congratulatory couple of days on a tropical island
in the Andaman Sea. When we get back, we'll begin putting the
footage together to see if it adds up to something interesting.

For now, I need a massage and a cocktail.

CASE FILE: *BIGFOOT*

NAMES: Bigfoot, Sasquatch, yeti, Migoi, Orang Pendek, Siberian Snowman, Skunk Ape, Yeren, Yowie, Almas.

DESCRIPTION: Descriptions vary by location, but the creature is often identified as a more-than-seven-foot-tall bipedal primate weighing up to one thousand pounds. Most witnesses report that the beast has thick, dark fur, broad ape-like facial features, and a massive frame. Some versions are described as emitting a strong, unpleasant odor or producing a distinct call.

LOCATIONS: Bigfoot is most commonly spotted in the Pacific Northwest of the United States as well as throughout British Columbia, Canada. Sightings of the yeti variant are also prevalent throughout the Himalaya mountain range in Asia. Additional iterations of the creature exist on every continent with the exception of Antarctica.

STATUS: In the pantheon of mystery creatures, there are legends and then there's the <u>legendary</u>. If cryptozoology has one undisputed Hall of Fame rock star, it has to be Bigfoot. The media darling of American cryptids, this seldom-seen primate is a bona fide global phenomenon. We witnessed the incredible magnitude of interest in the creature firsthand when our discovery of a print in Malaysia created international headlines. Known by dozens of names, Bigfoot has more alter egos than Peter Sellers.

Over the years, footprints have been the primary source of Bigfoot evidence. There are also hundreds of eyewitness accounts and an assortment of blurry photographs and amateur movies. Believers view the 1967 Patterson film as proof of the creature's existence, while Bigfoot's detractors claim it to be an indisputable hoax.

VERDICT: In considering the existence of Bigfoot, the eight-hundred-pound gorilla in the room is that there is no eight-hundred-pound gorilla. The simple fact that we have yet to find incontrovertible physical evidence of a creature as massive as Bigfoot living in the United States is probably telling. When you consider the countless hours spent in search of this creature, it's incredibly difficult to imagine that Bigfoot, not to mention a population of Bigfoots (Bigfeet?), could continue to elude documentation or capture.

I am slightly more inclined to consider the existence of the yeti, due to the sheer scope of the Himalayan wilderness and the virtually impenetrable terrain in which he is believed to live. There are more than 250 individual peaks here, including nine of the fifteen tallest mountains on earth. If a creature were able to adapt to such a vast, unforgiving environment, it might be able to evade human detection.

To me, the most plausible variation of the Bigfoot legend is a creature called the Orang Pendek. This stocky primate is reported to inhabit the dense jungles of Indonesia and has been described by hundreds of locals. These tangled forests collectively constitute an area the size of Vermont and are nearly impossible to access. Respected biologist Debbie Martyr has been stationed here for more than a decade studying elephants, rhino, and tigers. To date, she has seen only four tigers, two elephants, and zero rhino. In ten years. That's how difficult this environment is to explore. She also unabashedly believes in the existence of the Orang Pendek and claims to have seen it herself.

In the end, the most interesting aspect of man's search for Bigfoot is what it says about us as a species. That almost all cultures cleave to a Bigfoot legend isn't just coincidental, it's fundamental. Every culture wants to understand their origins, and Bigfoot has become a mysteriously universal archetype—a long-lost hirsute relative we yearn to know.

Are there still undiscovered populations of primates hiding on earth? Yes. In fact, in a staggering find, a new species of monkey was recently described in the tropical forests of Colombia. And two years ago researchers found 125,000 gorillas in the Republic of Congo that had gone unnoticed in the swampy rain forests. These types of discoveries suggest that there may be many other species yet to be catalogued. Still, it doesn't seem likely to me that the star of <u>Harry and the Hendersons</u> is going to emerge from the woods behind a Bed Bath & Beyond in Tacoma, Washington.

6: Post

Hollywood, California, 2006

For a postproduction neophyte, the process of editing the
pilot seems nearly as daunting as shooting it. Hundreds of
hours of footage from our impromptu expedition need to be
assembled and made coherent. It's a challenging process.
Editing, especially self-editing, can also be an exercise in
blistering frustration. Like a time machine, software has the
power to reshape the past, highlighting selective experiences
and coalescing them into something decidedly improved.
Adventure can be heightened, humor can be parsed, and
interviews can be condensed to their most vital elements. At
the same time I find myself helpless to change my own actions.
I now have questions for interviewees that I can no longer ask,
and I see missed opportunities at the corner of every frame.

One of the pitfalls of making docu-style television is
that it's easy to be tricked into thinking that your personal
experience is going to be shared by the viewer simply because
you're recording the events. But reality is highly subjective,
even to a camera. Put another way: Two people go out to
dinner at a seaside restaurant and are seated in a booth. One
person is seated facing the kitchen, while the other faces

the interior of the restaurant. One angle affords the harsh
fluorescent glow of the cramped service station and waiters
scraping half-eaten meals into the garbage. Another offers
a view of open space, candlelit tables, and a vista of waves
crashing in the background. The food in the middle is the
television show, and the two customers are the cameras.
Though the actual food they share is identical, only one will
relish the meal. It's a question of perspective. Even in "reality"
television, it's not enough to just film one's experience. It's
critical to voyeuristically consider it through the eyes of the
cameras. Did we get a close-up of that flickering lantern? Did
we establish a wide shot that shows just how crowded this
market is? Can we see that the interviewee is brandishing a
spear? All of the little things that make us feel a certain way
about a moment need to be accounted for. Otherwise, a scene
that was tense might feel casual to the viewer; a moment of
great adventure might read as pedestrian. Reality, it turns out,
needs to be presented very carefully.

After finishing a first cut of the show, our plaster trophy
in hand, we victoriously march over to SciFi like Perseus with
a Gorgon's head. The footprint cast is paraded in front of the
executives along with a half dozen newspaper articles from
overseas. It's a pretty impressive haul, especially given the
channel's realistic expectations of a team hunting a possibly
fictional monster.

The executives are thrilled with the pilot, which we edited
as a fairly earnest documentary on the Malaysian Bigfoot. Mark
Stern asks for an interesting adjustment, wanting to see more of
our actual travels, humor, and the logistical obstacles we faced
in the field. In other words, any efforts we made to scrub the

show into something shiny weren't nearly as interesting as the messy realities of the travel itself.

As we return to the edit bay, rather than approach the material from a distance, we shift our own experiences to center stage. As Vincent Chow told me in Malaysia, "The journey is what matters." We begin to include the bumpy roads, the bad food, and the broken engines, allowing the viewer to ride shotgun along the way. The final product is tremendously well received and offers the Channel a completely different animal to sit alongside *Ghost Hunters*. Before I know it, they order a first season of six one-hour episodes. "Keep your bags packed, Gates," Stern tells me.

And that's how a hapless adventurer suddenly became an international monster hunter. Since that pilot, my life has been inexorably changed. Over the next few years I will touch down in more than eighty countries around the world and conduct investigations into more than sixty mysterious creatures and phenomena.

In some ways it's very easy to look at the genesis of *Destination Truth* as an incredible stroke of good fortune. A lucky break. And, of course, that's true to a large extent. But beyond that, I've honestly come to feel as though my revelations on Kilimanjaro somehow catalyzed the journey that followed.

If travel has momentum and wants to stay in motion, as I mentioned earlier, then adventure has the gravitational pull of a black hole. The more you do it, the more you find a way to keep doing it. It becomes something vital to the system. Adventure rewrites the routine of our lives and wakes us sharply from the comforts of the familiar. It allows us to see how vast the expanse of our experiences can actually be. Our ability to grow is no longer linear but becomes unrestricted to any direction we wish to run. If Neil Mandt and *Destination Truth* weren't at the bottom of Kili, then I would have found another adventure altogether.

Lucky for me, though, the road brought me to an opportunity beyond my wildest dreams. And now I was getting that opportunity all over again.

And that's when things really got interesting.

7: Mixmaster Belong 'Em Jesus

Papua New Guinea, 2007

As we make our final approach to the airfield, a fit Aussie sporting a short-crop haircut leans over my shoulder to peer out the window. He's been sitting in silence since we took off from Brisbane three hours earlier. "Hi," he offers, still focused on the city below. "My name is Steve. I'll be keeping you alive down there."

We land and taxi to the dilapidated terminal. Outside, it's humid, wet, and dirty, as close to a proper introduction to Papua New Guinea as you can get. Its capital, Port Moresby, is like the Mos Eisley spaceport in *Star Wars*, except with significantly more scum and villainy. There are international cities in the world with worse reputations, I suppose, but not many. We leave the airport in an armored vehicle with reinforced steel slats over the windows, and I scan the edges of the road for what I can only assume is an impending zombie attack. The city is teeming with gang violence, and a carjacking here last week left three people dead. I encourage the driver to step on it.

Along the way, Steve reveals himself as an ex-military SAS officer contracted to provide private security for our expedition. He's also one hell of a nice guy. We bring him up to speed on our itinerary, which is slightly more organized than our outing to Malaysia. This is an unpredictable place, and Steve's presence here will be critical in navigating the intense local politics.

Despite the country's geographical coziness to Australia, Papua New Guinea remains fiercely independent and yet alarmingly non-nationalist. Locals are more apt to identify with their clan than with their fellow countrymen. Nine hundred tribal dialects, endless regional bickering, and a nearly broken political system: many would argue that the country is simply a failed state. Not one prime minister has completed a full five-year parliamentary term in the last *thirty years*. And with more than $400 million somehow gone missing from government coffers in the last decade, it's safe to say there might be a touch of corruption in the capital as well.

All of Port Moresby's deficits are a particular shame, since the rest of the country is one of the best adventure destinations on earth. This is a place where the long arm of tourism hasn't fully reached, where tribal culture prevails, and the rusted relics of World War II are still on full display. Plus, this tropical wonderland is brimming with uncataloged biodiversity. Each year dozens of new species are discovered in the nearly impenetrable jungles; scientists often refer to these archipelagos as a "lost world."

This is our first and most ambitious stop of the season. We've come here to investigate three cryptozoological fugitives: a mermaid that has been spotted near the Papuan island of New Ireland for generations, as well as two different living dinosaurs purported to inhabit nearby New Britain Island. As outlandish as these creatures might sound, PNG, as it's known, would certainly be the sort of place to harbor them.

We begin our investigation into the mermaid story, conducting a few interviews at the local university. Our time in the crime-stricken capital is thankfully brief, though, and before long we're off to the airport for our flight to New Ireland. The process of checking in is unabashed chaos. The concept of a line hasn't really caught on in this corner of the world, and every passenger on every Air Niugini flight simply mobs the counters from any available angle, waving his or her ticket in the air. We somehow manage to tag our bags, run down the tarmac, and board the plane.

The beat-up turboprop sputters up over the crystalline waters of the Bismarck Archipelago and the New Guinea Highlands. I gawk down at the virgin jungles with amazement. The more than one million people that inhabit this part of the country weren't even discovered by the outside world until the 1930s. There are whispers that cannibalism, popular here for centuries, may still be ritually practiced.

At the tiny airport in Kavieng, we step down from the plane and into the blistering sunshine. Our bags are taken out of the hold of the plane and simply strewn along the tarmac, along with a dead body. I hear wails and crying from locals pressed up against the chain-link fence at the arrivals terminal as the crude coffin is moved out of the heat. It's a distressing sight and a portentous introduction to the island.

After collecting our gear, we meet Lucas, our Papuan liaison, who is supposed to help facilitate our presence here. With his thick bristled moustache and short legs, he looks a little bit like Super Mario as he scampers across the tarmac, out of breath. His mouth and facial hair are covered in a thick bloodred juice, and just as he's about to shake my hand, he literally doubles over and drops to the ground with dizziness. This is my introduction to *buai*.

The chewing of this bizarre combination of ingredients is nothing short of a national addiction in PNG. Also immensely popular throughout the Pacific and Southeast Asia, *buai* is actually the fourth most consumed drug on the planet after nicotine, alcohol, and caffeine. A seemingly random recipe of betel nut, mustard stick, and lime (the chemical, not the fruit) is combined and chewed, producing torrential amounts of bright red saliva, which Papuans spit on just about every surface in sight. While it's used universally as a mild pick-me-up, its narcotic effects seem to render the population in a daze. I wait patiently for Lucas to regain his footing and look over as our pilot and copilot leave the aircraft; both men's mouths are stained red, and they spit liberally on the tarmac. I'm suddenly feeling lucky to have landed in one piece.

The jeeps we arranged aren't at the airstrip for some reason, but Lucas promises that they're en route. While we wait, Lucas introduces me to two local cops who will accompany us on the expedition. Steve and I exchange a wary look as the two men present themselves. Both have *buai* spit stains on their shirts, and neither looks much like a police officer. I ask one of them to show me his gun, which he unholsters and places in my hand. I look down at a rusted Smith & Wesson revolver that appears to have been pried out of the dead hand of Wyatt Earp. I pop open the ancient cylinder to discover that all of the chambers are empty. I ask him if he has any ammo, and he fishes through his breast pocket to produce a handful of loose change and two bullets. One isn't even the right caliber.

The jeeps finally arrive, but actually getting out of town is a challenge. I've experienced "island time" in my travels, but Papuans have taken ass dragging to a whole new level. It takes an hour to get the jeeps fueled and another hour to buy a few loaves of bread and bottled water. The estimated drive time to Nokon Village, the epicenter of supposed mermaid activity, is eleven hours, and we haven't even started. My watch reads 3:00 p.m. It isn't overly safe to drive through these jungles after dark, but we have little choice at this point. I'm just hopeful the local cops can use their one good bullet to put down any form of rebellion we might meet along the way.

The first few hours are a dream. Small villages glide by, and a riot of green rushes past the windows. Along the road, locals emerge from the brush, almost all of them carrying enormous machetes. Even the children are well armed. Still, they wave excitedly as we pass by, then recede in a cloud of dust and smiles. Eventually, however, the road falls apart, and we lose ten to fifteen kilometers per hour to absorb the bumps.

As darkness sets in, the machete-wielding villagers suddenly seem a bit more ominous when they appear in our headlight beams; most of the population retreats away from the road altogether. We finally call it quits in a nondescript village in the middle of God knows where. There's not much to see here, but we've been told there's a rough guesthouse to call home for the night. As we unload our gear into the basic cement rooms, I can hear a distant preacher yelling through a megaphone somewhere in the jungle. After settling in, we hit up what passes for a neighborhood bar, a thatched-roof hut with a transistor radio and a few wooden chairs. We gulp down warm South Pacific brand beers, and Neil and I throw a few rounds of darts onto a tattered board. The only food being served is some sort of mystery sausage that tastes gamey and dry. Possibly goat meat. But out here, who knows?

We eventually stroll back over to the guesthouse, tired, drunk, and happy. I stand on the porch looking out into the jungles, an empty beer bottle dangling between my fingers. Suddenly, every single light in the village clicks off. The whir of the town's only generator spins down to silence and is replaced by the stinging buzz of insects. The power is gone for the night. Even the preacher has called it quits. There's an immediacy to the stillness that's unnerving. I use a headlamp to navigate back to my room and drift off to sleep in the pitch-black night.

Up before the sun (and well before the generator), we pack quietly and hit the road—or what's left of it. By mid-morning we finally arrive in Nokon Village. We're totally off the grid now. There's no power, no running water, and only tribal law. Our jeeps are immediately swamped by machete-carrying locals who greet us warmly and welcome us to the village. Some of the children seem scared; no doubt they haven't seen many "dim dims," or white people, in these parts.

Steve acts as a vital go-between, since he can speak the native Tok Pisin, a pidgin English. For those who have never had the confused pleasure of encountering this hand-me-down language, it is genuinely bizarre. It consists largely of English words picked up by laborers and then repurposed throughout the Pacific as a unique language. Though the vocabulary sounds familiar, without an understanding of pidgin idioms, it's gibberish. For instance, a helicopter is called a "Mixmaster belong 'em Jesus." A "Mixmaster" is a blender with spinning blades and "belong 'em Jesus" refers to the fact that these aircraft seemingly appear from the heavens. To ask someone's age one would say, "How many Christmas you?" To move quickly is to "hariup" (hurry up). A "Do not disturb" sign would read "Yu no ken kam insait" (You cannot come inside). While Steve is translating, a local picks up a pair of our binoculars and calls them "glasses belong 'em kaptin," a reference to colonial sailors from centuries past. In short, the language is bonkers. I try to follow along, but half the time it sounds like they're drunk or talking shit about me.

We ask to speak to the village chief, who then comes loping out of a nearby grass hut. A stocky, white-haired old man with his mouth stained bright red and naturally, he's wearing a decades-old Donkey Kong baseball cap. Not exactly Hiawatha. Still, he's the elder of the community, and his favor is critical to our expedition. In PNG, even the elected officials defer to these traditional leaders. And considering the fifty machetes within our twenty-foot radius, if the boss here doesn't approve of our presence, we'll be leaving quickly. Fortunately, he's more than happy to see us, spitting a huge wad of saliva on the ground to smile broadly with his few remaining teeth. He leads us into the main village, a scattered collection of huts along a sandy beach. We sit with the villagers and discuss the mysterious sightings.

For years, people here have seen what we would call a mermaid, though the Papuans refer to it as a "Ri." Specifically, they see a figure bobbing at the surface of the water, which then descends beneath the waves. When pressed to actually describe the creature, however, the witnesses defer to the generic image of a beautiful nymph. The interviews illuminate one of the critical lessons learned while making *Destination*

Truth: that *truth* itself is relative. Our Western obsession with objectivity and demonstrable evidence holds little sway in certain cultures. Places like Papua New Guinea have sliding scales when it comes to the value and interpretation of events. In this community, oral tradition is sacrosanct, and a storyteller's narrative is *true* regardless of whether it's factual. There's little need for empirical evidence. It's simply not a part of their belief system.

We hear a story about a man in possession of mermaid bones that (unsurprisingly) turns out to be hard to confirm. We're then told that the bones are actually buried between two palm trees on the beach, and while I have little hope of finding anything, my team and I take turns digging, to the sheer delight of the locals. It's not that they don't believe in the creature: they absolutely do. Ardently. They just can't imagine why anyone would toil in the hot sun for evidence. The longer I dig, the more I agree with them.

Coming up empty-handed, we attempt to verify additional sightings by scuba diving in the waters of nearby Elizabeth Bay. We explore untouched corals and hover over the carcasses of massive troop transport boats from World War II. The underwater investigation, while breathtaking, yields no actual mermaid sightings.

Back onshore, however, we do see something significant bobbing at the surface, which, for an instant, appears humanoid. Careful observation reveals that it's something else entirely. The animal is a dugong: a marine mammal, relative of the manatee, and a strong candidate for what the locals are seeing. Additional research reveals that the dugong species is of the scientific order Sirenia. Sirenia are named for the Sirens of Greek mythology, since it is theorized that Mediterranean sailors historically mistook manatees as, you guessed it, mermaids. But the question remains: How did remote Papuans in the Pacific come to perfectly describe a creature from Greek mythology? The answer lies in the same cultural cross-pollination that makes pidgin such a bizarre hybrid language.

As the war's Pacific theater unfolded on Papua New Guinea's shores, the local population struggled to make sense of modern boats and futuristic-looking aircraft. Tribes famously created "cargo cults," believing that arriving food rations and military gear were actually from God and meant for the Papuans themselves. They believed the soldiers were intercepting these holy supplies, and, in an effort to cut out the middleman, locals hastily constructed useless boat docks and primitive airstrips in the hopes that more cargo would simply, well, show up. These coveted supplies offered clues to a world that these people never knew existed. Many shipments included cans of tuna fish, on which they would have noticed the same logo that persists on packaging to this day: a reclining mermaid. The villagers in PNG are simply carrying on a muddled tradition of misidentification as old as Homer himself. So the next time you're at the supermarket buying a can of Chicken of the Sea, take stock of the power of myth.

Satisfied at our explanation of the Papuan mermaid, we turn to face another creature on the nearby island of New Britain. The daylong drive back to the airport in Kavieng is going to knock us off schedule, so we decide to simply travel in a direct line, taking a boat between the two islands. I'm advised that the crossing can be rough and should be attempted just before dawn.

We wake up at 3:30 a.m. under the cover of darkness and haul our equipment down to the beach. It's pouring, and even with rain gear, we're drenched in minutes. I hike down over the rocks to get a look at the water; what I see is not overly encouraging. The ocean is dark and churning, and the banana boats the locals sourced don't look particularly seaworthy. We try to wait out the rain for another half hour, but it's relentless. Finally, we give it a go. We lash the gear under tarps and carry the boats to the water's edge. It's hard to tell if the ocean is getting worse or if the morning light is just revealing how bad the conditions really are. Either way, we don't last long. After struggling to make it across the breakers, Neil and I take a rogue wave to the face. About $10,000 worth of gear is destroyed in an instant. We return to shore. So much for the boat idea.

Back on land, we dry off as the sun begins to break. The ocean remains rough, and the swells are worse than ever. I ask the villagers if there's a field in the area. One of the locals guides us to an abandoned World War II airstrip. We tag the coordinates on GPS and fire up a satellite phone, eventually linking to a helicopter pilot on the other island. While we wait for a chopper, the locals paint my face using their stained saliva. It smells awful, but they're enjoying it too much for me to argue. Finally, we hear the sound of spinning blades and wave our arms at the approaching helicopter. Belong 'em Jesus, indeed.

I climb into the front compartment, the crew hops in the back, and away we go. As we gain altitude, the entire island steadily resolves into a tapestry of palm trees and thatched roofs. The Duke of York Islands roll by as we course above the frothy waves and deep blue sea. As we approach New Britain,

my eyes widen at plumes of menacing smoke that billow out
of three active volcanoes. We arc around one of the larger
cones, which, until fairly recently, was entirely underwater. In
the 1800s it exploded up from the depths, and when it finally
quieted, there was a new island here. Maps had to be redrawn.
The large town of Rabaul constructed shortly after was one
of PNG's most cosmopolitan but also an astonishingly poor
choice of real estate. In 1994 the inevitable finally happened.
A brutal eruption devastated Rabaul, with rocks the size of cars
raining down over the city and heavy ash crushing most of the
buildings. Today it is a chalky, abandoned ghost town resting
peacefully in the shadow of still-smoldering giants. Six hundred
feet away, a new Rabaul is springing up, unwilling to learn
from the mistakes of its past.

Our helicopter lands on the outskirts of the ruined city. We
are immediately presented with a hefty bill for our last-minute
helicopter extraction, which Neil and I promptly charge to the
network. We're here to search for an iguanodon-like dinosaur
that locals have reported seeing in the nearby jungles. Our
mission is straightforward: head to the remote village where the
creature was spotted, interview the locals, and attempt to figure
out what they saw.

We meet with the town mayor, who directs us out of town
and kindly insists on loaning us an additional security guard.
As the mayor diplomatically prattles on about how I'm going
to love the unspoiled rain forests and friendly natives, I can't
help but notice that my new escort is carrying a fully automatic
machine gun. We drive out of Rabaul past ash-covered ruins
on streets lined with charred palm trees. Above the blackened
foliage, I notice the volcano belch out a cloud of vapor and

cross my fingers that I'm not about to find myself in a Roland Emmerich movie.

After orchestrating the attack on Pearl Harbor, Admiral Isoroku Yamamoto moved his base of operations to Rabaul. By 1941, this entire island was overrun with more than 100,000 Japanese soldiers. Today there are still lingering reminders of this bloody past all around us. The natural vegetation is broken up by huge gun turrets and scattered mechanical debris. By the side of the road I notice a graveyard and a long-abandoned execution area. It's a disquieting sight and we continue on in silence.

The muddy road slits the jungle like a knife but becomes more and more compromised by the encroaching foliage. By the time we make it to our destination, the ground is barely visible. We step out of the jeeps into a clearing where I can make out a loose arrangement of huts. I also hear the sound of beating drums, which brings a smile to my face. We're about to be given a proper welcome. The villagers emerge, and we're surrounded by traditional painted dancers clad with necklaces of dried flowers. As the drumming picks up pace and the dancers encircle my team, I stand amazed at the vivid eruption of culture.

Since the whole scene feels a bit like the arrival at Skull Island in *King Kong*, we're doing our best to ingratiate ourselves. The quickest way to fit in here is also the simplest; my crew and I agree to partake in a mouthful of *buai*. As the entire village looks on in delight, we make an earnest if pathetic attempt to chew the nearly inedible betel nut as drool comes spilling out of our mouths. We spit the juice out onto the ground, which is already stained red as far as the eye can see. The power of the bitter concoction hits us first-timers like a ton of bricks, and within minutes we're all high as kites and stumbling around like a pack of fools. Marc Carter is dancing like a chicken, Neil is reeling and can barely stand, and the entire village laughs their collective ass off. For the next ten generations, they'll probably be talking about the white idiots who came to their village one day.

The effects pass quickly, and we're warmly embraced by the entire tribe. They serve us a challenging lunch of stewed bananas and taro root, which we diplomatically consume as best we can. I teach the kids how to use an iPod (it turns out that a click-wheel really is pretty intuitive); they squeal with laughter, tickled by the strange sounds of a little-known band called "the Beatles."

A tour of the village is revelatory. There's a vibrant community here that is totally divorced from the modern world. The discovery that the locals are still using seashells for currency is downright mind-blowing. I spend the better part of an hour trying to work out the dollars-to-shells conversion rate, but in the end I just give up. I'm offered a few thirteen-year-old brides, which I politely decline, as we weave our way between the simple huts and throngs of onlookers.

We get down to business and interview eyewitnesses who claim to have seen the iguanodon creature. They nearly universally describe the animal as having a dog-like head, a long body, and a spiked tail. Villagers seem to think it's a dinosaur of some sort. Several people claim that the creature has eaten local dogs. We also buy a live chicken to use for bait that the mayor strangles to death, a process at which he doesn't appear overly adept. The zombie chicken keeps coming back to life again and again, and I gnash my teeth waiting for it to be over.

Finally, with our (hopefully) dead chicken and a fan

club comprising everyone in town, we head out to begin our investigation. One eyewitness is actually too scared to descend the slope where she spied the creature. This is a little nerve-racking, since it's clear some kind of animal really did frighten this woman, iguanodon or not. A few of the locals assist in erecting a base camp, using machetes to create bamboo supports for our rain tarp. In the span of about three minutes, they turn the site into the Professor's hut from *Gilligan's Island*, fashioning a table, two chairs, and a roof out of bamboo, putting my own camp-building efforts to utter shame. I half expect them to install a coconut phone.

Just before dark, we string out a series of infrared cameras to survey the area for any movement. Thermal imagers aid our efforts as well, piercing the darkness and illuminating anything that emits heat. While part of the team begins a preliminary sweep, the rest of the group continues to activate the equipment at base camp.

The ensuing investigation is notable in that it marks the first of two instances when I nearly get my head blown off while making *Destination Truth*. It happens as we trudge through a swampy section of wilderness beyond our camp. I hack at a huge banana leaf that suddenly drops away to reveal a heavily cleared expanse and about twenty Papuans servicing construction equipment. The men immediately stop what they're doing and accost our group, hysterically yelling and waving us away. Two of the men are holding pistols, which they wave about haphazardly in the general direction of my face; the rest step forward with machetes. I watch our Papuan security guard take the safety off of his machine gun and I motion the muzzle down while Steve politely apologizes for the intrusion.

An argument ensues but is settled when we all back off from the site and agree to go around.

As we retreat, I glance back at the equipment, which appears to be dredging part of the swamp. Steve tells me that they're looking for the wreckage of an American bomber from World War II, which they believe was carrying a shipment of gold. Clearly, they're protective of the bounty.

We double back to base to begin our overnight investigation, more than a little wary of our newly discovered neighbors. I'm less than surprised to find that Lucas has fallen asleep on a log.

The rest of the night is monopolized by an extensive search of the jungles surrounding the village. Just after midnight, we encounter something that shakes the trees so hard I'm convinced it's the Smoke Monster from *Lost*. Whatever it is, we never get a good look, and it quickly flees into the darkness. We trek on and eventually loop back to our camp. The video monitors back at our bamboo base show flickering scenes of static jungle and a dead chicken swaying in the breeze.

At dawn there's little to report by way of findings, and the chicken is cooked and consumed by the villagers. Though our culprit is described as an iguanodon, the consistent elements from the interviews sound to me like this monster might be a large crocodile (of which Papua New Guinea has many).

We speed away from the village, waving back at a mob of cheering locals. Though we didn't find their dinosaur, this was certainly a journey of discovery for my group. Palm fronds smack the front bumper of our car, clawing at the doors before releasing us and cloaking the road behind. I wonder if I'll ever see this place again.

At the airstrip we board a flight to Lae, a city nestled in the Huon Gulf on the west side of the main Papuan island. We're flying in an old de Havilland Dash 7, a plane better suited for a museum than the friendly skies. A rattling old piece of junk, the plane lurches up off the tarmac and lets out a cacophony of ill-fated mechanical sounds. As we level out, I watch as the copilot props his knee against the stick and opens a local newspaper across his lap. The headline reads, "GIANT CROC KILLS LOCAL WOMAN." It seems the Iguanodon has struck again.

We're now on the hunt for Papua New Guinea's flying dinosaur. Known as the Ropen, this pterodactyl-like cryptid has been spotted in the skies over PNG for decades. The creature is said to be uniquely bioluminescent, glowing brightly as it flies. As the rusted wings of our plane shudder in the cloud line, we drop down toward the tarmac to begin the search.

The main airport here is in disrepair and closed, so we head for a World War II strip, which hasn't seen much service in the last fifty years. We somehow touch down in one piece and make our way to a primitive yet serviceable hotel. It's the first running water that we've seen in nearly a week. I shower quickly, and while the rest of the group cleans up, I grab the car keys and jump in the jeep. There's a place nearby that I've always wanted to go.

I step out at the old Lae airfield, which now sits in abject disrepair. I walk along the silent runway and crouch down, skimming my hand across the rough stones at my feet. It was here, in 1937, on the very pebbles that now slip between my fingers, that a heavily loaded Lockheed Electra plane gained momentum and took off into the blue. The pilot, a wiry, thirty-nine-year-old woman, was bound for tiny Howland Island, more than 2,500 miles away. But Amelia Earhart would never arrive. I rise to my feet and slowly walk the length of the narrow field, looking up at the clouds and picturing her waving to the locals before arcing out over the ocean. I'm fascinated by her, of course. What adventurer isn't? Her many exploits were brazen but undertaken with such surety of purpose that they appeared effortless. Earhart was seemingly unconstrained by gravity, an aviatrix Astaire who could glide across the globe with ease. During her trans-world flight, she wrote, "Please know I am quite aware of the hazards . . . I want to do it because I want to do it. Women must try to do things as men have tried. When they fail, their failure must be but a challenge to others."

The magnificent thing about her is, in the eyes of the world, she simply never died. Her fear never witnessed, her failure never recorded, her shiny twin-engine Electra never recovered. Earhart's legacy of inspiration is amplified because her adventure is perpetual. We don't think of her as dead; we think of her as missing. She is forever flying, somewhere beyond Lae, over that limitless blue horizon.

I head back to town and to our comparatively modest adventure. The most recent sightings of the Ropen are concentrated along a small peninsula that we can only access by boat. I pilot one of two vessels, hugging the coast and riding the swells toward our target. We bank in toward a simple village, noticeable only by small fires set along the beach. We tie up at a primitive dock and begin to interview the witnesses. All of them describe a large, bat-like monster and then point up to the sky, recalling the Ropen's strange glow. They gesture toward the jungles along the coast. The entire peninsula they're referring to is now a nearly impenetrable mess of vegetation, snakes, and spiders. We look over wartime maps to see that, like in Rabaul, the Japanese did a thorough job of turning this particular sliver of land into a military powerhouse. Dozens of gun turrets are marked on the documents, as well as a vast network of defensive tunnels that underlie the entire area. Allied forces bombed the region so heavily that the Japanese spent much of their occupation underground. The locals believe that the Ropen now inhabits these tunnels.

Our first attempt at exploring the forest is by way of direct assault. We leave the beach, passing a perfectly preserved Japanese Zero plane that's literally hanging out of a tree. The path degrades quickly, and we eventually reach a dead end. We revisit the maps, and the locals point out a nearby feature that we've missed: the entrance to a tunnel. They cut back vines to reveal a badly collapsed opening that's now completely sealed. We translate back and forth between pidgin and English and are told that an earthquake destroyed the opening more than fifty years ago.

"How many people can you get together from the village?" Neil asks Lucas.

"Neil?" I interject. Even though I know exactly what he's thinking.

"What? You'll love it in there," he offers smugly.

While Neil oversees the work of uncovering the tunnel entrance, I lead the rest of our group on a trail up the peninsula, searching for an alternate entrance. The heat is absolutely sweltering as we trek uphill, and by the time we reach the first Japanese gun turret, my clothes are soaked through. I sit behind the rusted barrel of the gun and look out through the natural camouflage of the canopy, imagining

Allied ships in the distance. We press on as far as we can, but hordes of prickly vines and spiderwebs prevent much progress.

Back near the beach, we come across a forgotten graveyard. Here the final resting places of gold miners, soldiers, and wayward travelers are being reclaimed by nature. Some of the plots are dug up and empty. The locals say that they believe this to be the work of the flesh-feasting Ropen, though to me simple grave robbery seems a much more likely cause. Names are still legible on a number of the broken headstones, and I walk down the line reciting them aloud. "Jack Davies. Charles Collins. Keith Suttor." I falter when I see a postscript under one soldier's name that reads, "KILLED BY NATIVE ARROW."

We hike back to the tunnel, where a hardworking team of locals has breached a small opening. With daylight fading, Carter and I wedge ourselves into the lightless cavity. We get to our feet, stooping forward under the low ceiling. The air is stale but breathable, and our headlamps illuminate crumbling walls and endless passages. To my dismay, we also find bats. Lots of bats. They whip through the chambers at high speeds and rush past our faces. We walk slowly and deliberately so that their echolocation can guide them around us (the best way to take a bat in the face is to panic and move quickly). Entire branches of the tunnel are collapsed, and we do our best not to think about how stupid an idea this is. Just keep moving. The sides of the tunnel are wet and flake to the touch. "Stay off the walls, Carter. They're falling apart," I whisper.

"Shit. Spiders," he answers.

I look back at Carter's headlamp beam, which illuminates the stocky legs of a tarantula drawing back into a hole. I scan the floor in front of me and see hundreds of glinting eyes retracting in the darkness.

The tunnel opens up a bit, and we come across railroad tracks originally used to deliver munitions to the guns on the hillside. I'm now adding unexploded ordnance to the list of things in here that could potentially kill us. We discover a few pieces of bone that look human but no signs of anything the size of a flying dinosaur. Once we've explored everything we can, we carefully pull back to the entrance. Neil and Eric pull Carter and me out of the hole and into the jungle darkness. The fresh air is a relief, and we sit on the ground for a few moments to catch our breath.

Our investigation continues throughout the night, and a few hours before dawn we, like so many others before us, do see strange lights. A small glowing ball appears low in the sky and streams slowly and steadily above the water. Since planes don't fly here after dark, it's not an aircraft, but I'm certainly not willing to concede that it's a flying dinosaur, either. The event is captured on our infrared cameras and we continue to scan the skies until sunrise, but the light never reappears. While the footage is ultimately inconclusive, it does align with eyewitness testimony, leaving the case open for future investigation.

At dawn, we return to Port Moresby and board a flight bound for home. In the end, it's hard to define PNG, and perhaps that's what makes it so special. It is at once a sprawling scrap yard from the Second World War, a treasure trove of unknown biodiversity, and home to tribal cultures that have staved off the modern age. It is dirty and yet pristine, both criminally corrupt and blissfully pure, and brimming with ways to kill you.

On the margins of antique maritime maps, cartographers would often write, "Here be monsters." It was a way of both warning and luring sailors to places unknown and uncharted. Papua New Guinea is such a destination, even today. Its highlands are barely explored and its jungles are among the wildest on earth. Its monsters come in many forms, from mermaids, iguanodons, and Ropens to crocodiles, spiders, and machete-carrying mercenaries. Some are folkloric and some all too real. Either way, though, the Papuans don't much care. To them, these are all indelible inhabitants of this mysterious lost world.

Here be monsters. Find them if you dare.

CASE FILE: *LIVING DINOSAURS*

NAMES: *Mokèlé-Mbèmbé, Emela-ntouka, Ninki-Nanka, Ngoubou, Mbielu-Mbielu-Mbielu, Nguma-monene, Arica Monster, Papuan iguanodon, Burrunjor.*

DESCRIPTION: *They are described as large (some in excess of thirty feet), dangerous, and decidedly prehistoric. They make up a category of cryptid that also includes T. rex, velociraptors, and an assortment of other dinosaur-like predators that somehow survived when the universe hit the control-alt-delete buttons on their existence.*

LOCATIONS: *These oversized creatures are primarily reported in the swamps of Central Africa. Additional sightings occur in locations as varied as the Australian Outback, the jungles of Papua New Guinea, and Chile's Atacama Desert.*

STATUS: *The nineteenth century prickled with a new awareness of and fascination with the unknown. Some of the most famous explorers of all time wandered the globe during these years. In Latin America: Alexander von Humboldt. U.S.: Lewis and Clark. Africa: Livingstone, I presume. And countless polar expeditions to boot. As a result, public interest in undiscovered lands and tales of faraway monsters was piqued, and the imagination of authors was sparked, creating an entirely new breed of adventure fiction. H. Rider Haggard made a five-shilling bet with his brother that he could write a book half as good as* Treasure Island *and published* King Solomon's Mines *in 1885 (ah, sibling rivalry). It quickly became a sensation. Once Sir*

Arthur Conan Doyle and Edgar Rice Burroughs penned _The Lost World_ and _The Land That Time Forgot_, respectively, man and dinosaur were forever destined to coexist on the pages of popular fiction.

What this interest truly amounted to, however, was an undeniable fixation with exoticism that further propelled explorers to pursue these creatures. Africa is ground zero in cryptozoologists' obsessive search for living dinosaurs. In the last one hundred years alone, nearly thirty expeditions have been dispatched to document the giant sauropod Mokèlé-Mbèmbé. These investigations, in some of the wildest parts of Africa, have resulted in amazing stories but little in the way of compelling proof. Nothing tops the story from a zoologist claiming he observed the creature for twenty minutes but was so excited he forgot to remove the lens cap from his camera. _Cough, cough. Bullshit._

VERDICT: In the case of another African monster known as the Emela-ntouka, when local tribesmen were shown photos of rhinos, many identified them as . . . Emela-ntouka. It's not uncommon. Many of these cryptozoological creatures are simply normal animals that have been magnified by native folklore over generations. The stories have been retold so many times that what we may have here is a simple failure to communicate.

There are places on earth where isolation has resulted in evolutionary diversions; the Galapagos Islands, Madagascar, and Papua New Guinea come to mind. However, a blue-footed booby is one thing; Grumpy from _Land of the Lost_ is quite another. We're not talking about a little poison dart frog, or an ivory-billed woodpecker here, but colossal, glass-of-water-vibrating, jeep-flipping, lawyer-eating dinosaurs. It would be impossible for these beasts to escape detection. So that's kind of a problem.

Let's face it. Everyone loves dinosaurs, and from Barney to Dino, our kids are downright obsessed with them. Their size, their majesty, and their incredible power . . . the only thing about dinosaurs that isn't awesome is the part where they all went extinct. To me, the case for living dinosaurs is merely mankind desperately wishing it were so. Our planet had previous tenants, and we'd love to meet them. So if you really want to run into a dinosaur, may I recommend the dusty fiction of Doyle, Burroughs, or even Crichton. You're guaranteed to find exactly what you're looking for.

8: Under New Management

Hollywood, 2007

Our exploits in Malaysia and Papua New Guinea gave way
to a voyage that unfurled across the globe. We traveled on to
Thailand, South Africa, Chile, and Argentina, searching for
evidence of strange creatures and paranormal phenomena
along the way. We tackled twelve individual stories, which
were then distilled into six hour-long episodes. The collective
experience was a nonstop thrill ride to film and a hard-knock
education on how to hunt monsters and make a television show
at the same time. This first season has since been released on
DVD. Even though it's a little rough around the edges, as I
look back on the journey now, I'm amazed at what we were
able to accomplish and how far we've come since then.

Though my journals from this inaugural season are
brimming with colorful tales of misadventure, it was our
travels through Malaysia and Papua New Guinea that stand
out for me as the best embodiment of the unscripted and
unpredictable nature of *Destination Truth*. After all, we traipsed
through some of the planet's most harrowing environments
and let the ensuing adventures dictate our story. It's supremely
difficult to make television this way, to stake a narrative on the

idea that interesting things will happen simply because the world is an interesting place. I'm just glad that it worked out and nobody lost a limb.

In Los Angeles, the long process of postproduction results in a unique series in SciFi's lineup. The show combines the investigative elements that fans of the immensely popular *Ghost Hunters* franchise already love but places those investigations in a totally different context; the final product is a fast-paced mash-up of travel, comedy, myth, and mystery.

A month before we're scheduled to air, I'm sitting at home watching Kevin Costner's award-winning performance in *Waterworld* on SciFi. For those who managed to miss this cinematic gem, it's basically about a guy with gills who drinks his own pee and occasionally clubs Jeanne Tripplehorn with an oar. There are also people on Jet Skis. At any rate, the movie goes to commercial, and I'm suddenly looking at a montage of myself. I do a full-spit take into my ficus plant and then sit bug-eyed while a deep-voiced announcer plugs *Destination Truth*. At the end of the commercial, a snappy logo pops up and everything. It's surreal. Beyond surreal. I even sit through the last act of *Waterworld* to see if it happens again.

The show premieres on June 6, 2007. It's one of the only SciFi shows ever positioned in the ten o'clock hour that holds on to a large percentage of *Ghost Hunters'* impressive audience. We're a hit! In response, the Channel orders more episodes, but unfortunately, Neil declines to produce the show himself. It sounds like there should be a juicy story here, but there really isn't. Neil and the Channel just can't reach an agreement. It's a huge loss to me, since Neil seems like the only person I know who's crazy enough to pull this series off.

His departure also means that we have to re-staff from top to bottom. I part ways with Carter, Eric, and the rest of the first-season team. It's bittersweet and feels a lot like starting over.

The Channel recommends that I meet with a producer named Brad Kuhlman, who worked with SciFi two years prior on a series called *Master Blasters* and had recently executive-produced *1,000 Places to See Before You Die* for the Travel Channel. He's the owner of a burgeoning production company called Ping Pong Productions that he runs with his best friend and business partner, Casey Brumels.

Brad and I arrange to meet at a restaurant in Hollywood. I arrive first, get a table, and nervously watch the door. I feel like I'm on a blind date, worried that Carrot Top is about to show up. After all, running around the world searching for monsters is a pretty close-quarters business, and it's really important to do it with people that you like and respect (or, at the very least, can tolerate). Brad steps in a few minutes later, and I have a hard time sizing him up. On one hand, he valets an obnoxiously huge Lincoln Navigator outside and is sporting hipster sunglasses and trendy sneakers. On the other hand, he seems completely down-to-earth. I sense that he's just as unsure of what to make of me, and we do our best to not scare each other off in the first few minutes. As it turns out, he's a great guy. By the time our entrées arrive, we're chatting like friends. He's experienced, funny, listens well (a quality I lack, so I always admire it in others), and has a genuine passion for travel.

A few days later, we meet again at a Borders bookstore, this time with Casey. I have no idea why we choose this location. Casey is significantly taller than Brad, with blond hair and a big, goofy smile. He's also immediately likable. It's easy to see why they're friends. Casey seems similarly engaged by the project, and it's clear that everyone is on board to work together. We sit amidst the paperbacks, spitballing potential locations for the second season and how best to evolve the show.

If there's one thing of which I'm unconvinced, it's whether these two understand just how hard *D.T.* is to make. They're both a bit cavalier about the whole thing at first; more than anything, they seem to think that it's going to be a lot of fun. Which it is, of course, but mostly in the way a plane crash is fun to reminisce about after you survive it. I do my best to explain the unique challenges of *Destination Truth* and to let them know how exhausting it is to film. I explain that the production is basically nonstop. Every aspect of our travels is filmed, and there's little time to rest. The accommodations are crappy, the food is worse, and the dangers are real. They grin and nod, unmoved by my gloomy prophecies. Ah, well. It doesn't really matter, I suppose. They'll both find out the truth soon enough. I just hope they pack something warm.

9: The Death Worm

Outer Mongolia, 2007

Despite once controlling the largest land empire in history, the great Mongol dynasty that once flourished has long receded, and the Mongolian people have been in something of a rut for the last seven hundred years. But now, finally free from the shackles of Manchurian and Soviet control, the frontier city of Ulaanbaatar is in the midst of an industrial revolution. Home to about a million people, the city cradles half the population of this sprawling country. Cranes and girders stretch up from the crowded, dusty streets. A new culture is emerging that's modern, stylish, and robust. But the evolution is slow. Infrastructure is lacking, the food is just plain awful, and the nightlife leaves something to be desired. Believe me, this is not the world's next spring break hot spot. Beyond the bounds of the city, the roads quickly decay and give way to the vast Gobi Desert, where the trappings of the modern world haven't yet infringed on centuries of traditional existence.

Swerve. I'm jolted awake as we skid around another washout in the road. A cloud of dust flies through the headlight beams and over the windshield. We left Ulaanbaatar at three a.m. We've been driving south for almost twenty hours, and

my knees can't take much more abuse against the dashboard.
Here, there is no road to follow, and the Land Rover carves
an undulating ribbon of sand around the steep ravines and
ancient, dried-up riverbeds. I've taken a break from driving and
can hardly keep my eyes open as I stare at the GPS receiver,
which is crudely duct-taped to the windshield. We've run out
of daylight and are now depending on satellites to guide us to
Dalanzadgad. Our new camera operator, Erica, and our audio
technician, Ponch, both shift around in the back, bundled in
down jackets to stave off the frigid cold leaching in through
the dark windows. The rest of the car—almost every square
inch—is occupied by equipment and supplies. Batteries,
cables, duffels, and hard cases sit democratically alongside
bags of beef, salami, peanuts, and bottles of water. I can hear
the external tanks of benzene sloshing around on the roof rack
above me, next to a spare set of tires.

We were supposed to arrive hours ago, but the convoy is
slower than expected. In the two vehicles behind us, I assume
that Brad, Casey, our new field producer, Araceli, and our tech
manager, T-Bone, are suffering an uncomfortable welcome to
their tenure on *Destination Truth*. The GPS glows out another
course correction as we turn our wheels into the smooth
grooves of a rutted track, the remnants of some abandoned road
to nowhere. I drift off to sleep.

As I'm the only member left from the original team, the
past months have been filled with endless new responsibilities.
In some ways it's been much easier. I've been newly integrated
as a producer and have taken a leading role in shaping our
stories and destinations. On the other hand, as I look out at the

frigid tundra of Mongolia, I'm realizing that I now have no one to blame for this awful drive but myself.

The Death Worm, known locally as Olgoi-Khorkhoi, is a nasty cryptozoological creature rumored to reside somewhere in these endless sands. The name translates as "intestine worm," owing to its long, segmented shape. Described as vividly red, the animal measures somewhere between three and five feet long. Details on its offensive abilities are varied and confusing, but the Worm is widely rumored to spit some sort of deadly acid at prey and dispence an immense electric charge when provoked. The attributes are so outlandish that it might hardly seem worth the effort to mount a search. What makes this creature intriguing, though, is the breadth of belief in its existence. Even though Mongolia is one of the least densely populated nations on earth, residents scattered across more than 600,000 square miles of desert are universally versed in tales of the Death Worm. This is a narrative that has transcended distance and time, passed down for generations.

The earlier part of the day was fascinating. Every so often we'd see a small cluster of yurts, the ghostly white outlines of these circular tents dotting the monotonous canvas of sand. We stopped in several of these nomadic enclaves to interview herders. It was hard to stomach the heated goat's milk or the salted meats that were presented to us, but offerings from people whose resources are so limited are not to be dismissed. They urged us to sit on the floor and warm ourselves around the tent's central stove. Firelight, it seems, is a universal kindle for storytelling, and as we huddled by the embers, legends gently glowed to life. They vividly recounted tales of the Olgoi-

Khorkhoi, even whispering the creature's name for added
theatrical effect.

My head eventually cracks against the window, and I
come awake fully. We've stopped. I peer through the frosted
glass and see nothing but the void. The driver opens his door
as an electrifying rush of cold overtakes the car's interior. I pull
my parka around me and hop out into the darkness, swearing
under my breath. The cars behind are stopping as well. Doors
open and the crew steps out to stretch their stiff legs. The hood
of our Land Rover is propped up, and I can see that one of
the drivers is trying to fix the stripped wiring on a headlamp.
I also notice something much more troubling: the rest of our
local escorts are carefully studying a map, bewildered. Our
main guide, Zanjan, who has been driving the second vehicle
in the convoy, looks dead on his feet. He opens a canteen of
water and, despite the subfreezing temperature, pours it over
his head, waking himself up. I glance over at Brad, who looks
beyond horrified.

"Zanjan, where the hell are we?" Brad demands.

"Close. We're close," Zanjan quietly replies.

"How close, Zanjan?" I say, now studying the map for
myself.

"Maybe another two or three hours," he admits.

This is not the answer for which the group is hoping.
An eruption of protestation follows, but it's for naught. We
are where we are, and it is what it is, a common mantra on
Destination Truth. We use the rooftop canisters to top off the
fuel supply, climb back into the Land Rovers, and carry on.

The final push is a blur to me. I fall asleep for seconds at
a time, vivid images and flashes of dreams spraying across the

inside of my eyelids. We bash through ditches and lurch over rocky hills for what seems like an eternity. The ordeal comes to an end at about two a.m. when the few, dim lights of the southern city of Dalanzadgad appear in the distance. A full twenty-two hours of off-road driving has left the entire team silent and sore.

We shuffle into a bleak-looking cement building that serves as a local hotel. Behind the desk are two young kids, both shitfaced, one cross-eyed. They're almost too loaded to check us in. I just walk behind the desk, snag a key off a hook, and shuffle upstairs into my chilly room, where I immediately collapse.

The sun rises entirely too soon, and I wake up feeling like I've been worked over by a baseball bat. At seven a.m. I limp downstairs, hunting for breakfast, and notice one of the kids from the front desk sitting alone in the kitchen chugging his morning Sapporo. Breakfast of champions. Outside, daylight reveals a grid of drab city streets that converge at a crumbling, dried-up fountain. The only residents I bump into are a few cows that pause to regard me with indifference as they amble through the center of town. There are entirely too many buildings here, considering the lack of people, which gives the place a feeling of abandonment. It's like I just wandered into a George Romero movie.

We conduct a series of interviews with townspeople (once we find them), meeting one man in a surreal bar called The Gobi Bear. The walls are lined with bear masks and glass cases filled with dried bear dung. The bartender is playing checkers with himself, and there's even a poster of Christina Aguilera holding her boob and giving the finger. The bar immediately jumps to number four on my list of world's best watering holes (the current standard-bearer is a beach bar in Zanzibar with a chained monkey behind the counter that tries to bite customers).

The residents here are no less impassioned storytellers than their nomadic brethren, and we repeatedly hear that there have been sightings of the Worm in abandoned ruins to the west. We set off deeper into the desert to pursue the most recent accounts.

We leave the town in a trail of dust, driving past primordial rock formations and through vast valleys of sand, traversing the deserts between here and the distant town of Gurvantes, more than two hundred kilometers away. We eventually come across another group of yurts where a herder and his wife emerge in thick fur hats and old, colorful robes.

They invite us inside a tent so welcoming that it's worth enduring the smell. A few snorts of the nomad's snuff help to banish the cold. I share a meal of sheep guts with their seven-year-old daughter and her elderly grandmother. The warmth they exude starkly contrasts the icy weather around them. Though their entire world is contained within the sloping domain of this simple tent, these nomads are so full of character and pride. They carry themselves like royalty, the deep lines on their faces the beautiful evidence of lives spent hard at work.

Today they're moving their home for the winter. We head outside, and I watch in amazement as the family breaks down their large, semi-rigid structure in less than thirty minutes flat. Every member of the family joins in the work. The seven-year-old hauls support poles, Mom breaks down the stove, Grandmother gathers up the heavy rugs, and Dad loads up the back of a Soviet-era truck. They will escort their material possessions across the desert to a winter camp offering better protection against the coming snows. The backbreaking work is enough to shame any American family who argues over taking out the trash.

While the last of their cargo is being tied down, the father tells me that, since I'm here hunting creatures, he wants to show me the remains of a "monster" that he's discovered nearby. The man leads us up a rise in the sand to a seemingly anonymous spot. There, I crouch down and see that he's camouflaged a patch of earth with a sand-covered tarp. I help him pull away the fabric and am confronted with an amazing sight: the fossilized skeleton of a dinosaur. We excavate part of the skull and jaw of what looks like some sort of raptor, although I can't be sure. Our efforts are interrupted by the honking horn of the fully loaded transport truck below. We leave the remains in place, to be reclaimed by the shifting sands and lost again in time.

Eventually we make it to the ruins where the Death Worm is said to reside. The area is abandoned now but was once a thriving Buddhist community destroyed under Communist rule. Today it is merely an open expanse framed by a few crumbled buildings and a steep rise in the distance. A frozen river bisects the plains, and a few small yurts will serve as our accommodations for the night.

The investigation that follows is one of the hardest and most miserable in *Destination Truth* history. After all, this is a newly formed team with little experience operating a unique set of equipment. Everything is trial and error. Mostly error. Plus, the conditions are so bitterly cold that even the most basic tasks seem to take forever. As with most of our investigations, a base camp is established; it serves as our surveillance hub.

From this central point, cameras are strung out into the field
to observe the perimeter and detect motion. Sweep teams are
dispatched with powerful night-vision scopes and high-tech
thermal imagers to conduct a more focused search.

On this particular night, nothing wants to work. The
video cables are nearly frozen solid, the thermal imager is
uncooperative, and our many batteries are quickly sapped by
the cold, causing one piece of equipment after another to shut
down. The good news is that the team is up to the challenge,
and we do our best to get the job done.

We cover every inch of the site, sending teams along and
across the frozen river and through every derelict block of
buildings. We take soil samples, send cameras down holes, and
carefully look for material evidence. We find little to support
a case for the creature. By now it's clear to me that the story
of the Death Worm is simply an heirloom, a legend carefully
handed down like a grandfather's pocket watch. By two a.m.
our last battery freezes to death, and the rest of us aren't far
behind. Our tech manager performs solemn funerals for several
hypothermic pieces of gear; it's time to call it quits.

We retreat into the three yurts, which are alarmingly
cold. Brad invites me over to his tent, where Casey has found
a few bottles of the local "Chingis Vodka," but I'm too tired
to celebrate. Plus, the thought of driving all the way back to
Ulaanbaator with a hangover seems like a fate worse than death.

The central stove in my yurt is stoked with a few scraps of
wood, but most of the fuel comes in the form of hardened cow
shit. The dung burns but doesn't give off much heat, which is
why it's so damned freezing in here. I load the patties into the
furnace and choose a cot along the wall. Along with a few thin

blankets, I find a discolored old sleeping bag labeled "Navajo Basic." I shiver inside of its paltry lining, realizing that what I really need is an "Eskimo Deluxe." Our medic and my current roommate, Ray, is snoring, and next door I can hear Brad, Casey, and Araceli laughing and drinking. It's a good sign. This night would have broken some people. I stare at the ceiling for a while, listening to the crackling stove and watching the firelight dance off the slanted wooden beams. Eventually I drift off to sleep, only to be startled awake hours later by the firm grasp of cold. I shuffle over to the stove, which is dead. The entire bucket of dung has vanished. A smile crosses my face as I realize that Brad and Casey must have robbed me in the night. I consider returning the favor as I step out into the darkness, but seeing as their chimney is almost out of smoke, there's probably not much left to steal.

Outside, the land is still and endless. I can see the stars wheeling and a thick band of the Milky Way gashing across the dome of sky. This one moment justifies all that has come before.

The reward for the effort required to reach the ends of the earth is often the simple satisfaction of being there by yourself. People seldom travel beyond civilization. It's a pity, since being alone in these barren destinations makes us feel our surroundings so acutely. When we can stand in the solitary presence of something magnificent, the obligation of sharing the experience evaporates, and we are free to truly be a part of it. Though we are insignificant in comparison, rarely in these moments do we feel overwhelmed. It's not about power. Whatever energy makes up this awe-inspiring world is the same stuff that courses inside all of us. These are the moments that reconnect us to our innate dignity.

I slowly close my eyes, reflecting on my position and imagining a bird's-eye view of our tents receding skyward as the panorama widens. I can see the last white smoke from the chimney rise up, and the desert around us stretching for more than a thousand miles. My mind's eye backs all the way up through the clouds as the curvature of the continent comes into frame. Ulaanbaatar, Beijing, Seoul, and Tokyo, lit up like so many suns. And with the earth now in full frame, I can still imagine our little tents, countless miles below, perched in the empty expanse. I open my eyes. I'm shaking cold but alive. Utterly alive.

CASE FILE: *PHANTOM FELINES*

NAMES: *Alien Big Cats, Mngwa, Blue Mountains Panther, Gippsland Big Cat, Tantanoola Tiger, Tasmanian tiger, Beast of Dartmoor.*

DESCRIPTION: *These are mysterious, predatory cats believed to be both intelligent and elusive, as evidenced by their ability to survive almost undetected. They can be separated into three categories: known living animals, true cryptozoological creatures, and those considered extinct.*

LOCATIONS: *England, Western Europe, East Africa, Australia, Tasmania, Papua New Guinea.*

STATUS: *Contrary to the name, Alien Big Cats are not felines from outer space that have come here to conduct anal probes. They are rogue animals that purportedly migrated beyond their original habitats and survived in anonymity for generations. In England, a growing number of citizens are adamant that uncataloged "ABCs" roam free across the countryside. Bolstered by hundreds of sightings, compelling photo and video evidence, and scores of unexplained livestock maulings, proponents of the existence of these colossal cats continue to pressure the media and government to investigate.*

In the case of the Mngwa in East Africa, the animal is rumored to be an undiscovered species that has somehow avoided being captured, killed, or documented. Many reports of this animal describe it as similar to a lion or leopard but larger, and covered with gray striped fur. The creature has mystified Western explorers for years. But to local tribesmen, it is simply an additional resident in the rich and deadly African menagerie.

The Tasmanian tiger (or thylacine) isn't actually a feline at all; it's a marsupial. The connection comes from its dark stripes and elongated tail, which are reminiscent of a big cat's. For thousands of years, this animal roamed the sprawling jungles of Australia, Tasmania, and Papua New Guinea. But after the introduction of aggressive species like the dingo and ruthless bounty hunting, the creature was eventually driven to the brink. On September 7, 1936, the last known thylacine died in captivity, a victim of careless neglect. In the decades since its demise, hundreds of eyewitness sightings have accumulated, and some believe that this predator is still alive, hidden deep in the jungles of Tasmania. Consider this creature the Elvis Presley of cryptozoology.

VERDICT: In terms of Europe's Alien Big Cats, I think the case is far from closed. Since large feline predators <u>have</u> been both captured and killed in rural England, some of these cats may be escapees from private breeders. It's very possible that fugitive kitties still linger in rural areas.

Having personally searched for the Mngwa, I'm not overly confident that it's about to pounce out of the tall grass anytime soon. A beast this ferocious is unlikely to spend his existence as a hermit. The Mngwa may simply be an oddly colored leopard or just a misidentified lion.

Reports of the Tasmanian tiger are enticing. While I'd be thrilled to learn that the species has prevailed, I think it's more probable that we won't see its kind again. Furthermore, without strict conservation efforts, other species like the thylacine will continue to vanish at alarming rates.

10: The Delicate Art
of Not Getting Killed

Halong Bay is a dreamscape. Endless emerald waters punctured by hundreds of limestone towers rising up like bony fingers from the deep. In a place this mysterious and enchanting, it's easy to understand how people could believe in a fantastical sea creature.

We've come to search for Vietnam's version of Nessie. Extracting the zoology from the mythology is one of the most challenging aspects of making *Destination Truth*, and this case is about as tough as it gets. Vietnam's history is laden with rich and imaginative folklore, including the elegant notion that a dragon descended from the heavens, his tail splitting the earth to form the jagged towers in the waters of Halong Bay. Even the name "Halong" means "where the dragon meets the sea." An alternate version has the dragon spitting out jewels, which formed the many islands here. Either way, these people have serpents on the brain, and reliable accounts are hard to come by.

Our boat, a massive wooden live-aboard on its maiden voyage, steams steadily between the monolithic karsts, a dragon's head rather appropriately carved into the prow. On deck, we set up cameras and equipment, prep dive gear, and scan the horizon. I glance back over the stern and furrow my brow at the sun, which is dropping like a heavy marble in the western sky.

Without warning, a series of hits on our sonar system sends us scrambling to get wet. Tapping the glass on the pressure gauge of my scuba regulator, I look down into the water, which I can already tell is going to be murky as hell.

My father spent the lion's share of his career as a commercial deep-sea diver, and I was tinkering with scuba tanks, weight belts, and wetsuits as far back as I can remember. Add to that a childhood by the sea in New England, and nautical exploits were something of a foregone conclusion for me. I've been diving since I was about ten years old, so young that after completing the Professional Association of Diving Instructors (PADI) open-water diving course I didn't qualify for a certification card. My earliest dives were icy shore excursions in Massachusetts, where the water perpetually feels like it drifted down from the Arctic Circle. My best friend Jon and I would don thick wetsuits to search for sunken treasure and undersea intrigue along the coast of Cape Ann.

One day, inspired by my father, I even tried to build a submarine out of a box fan and a metal firewood rack. Needless to say, my personal *Nautilus* suffered an inglorious end, promptly disassembling and sinking at her modest launching ceremony. Even at the age of twelve, Jon wasn't one to pull punches as we watched my Vernian contraption gurgle to the bottom of the bay. "Idiot," he quietly muttered. Little did either of us know that professional sea monster hunting would end up on my résumé.

Jumping into Halong Bay feels like a bad idea from the start. The dire reminder from the director of the zoological museum that these waters are populated with venomous sea snakes engages me in a mental battle as I imagine what exactly triggered the sonar beneath the boat. Visions of tentacles dance in my head. It doesn't help that we've got limited control over our environment, with curious boats recklessly swinging by to get a better look at what we're up to. It's not exactly an ideal dive profile.

Casey and I jump down into the warm waters and are immediately engulfed in a blinding broth of mud and silt. We try to get our bearings, but the fact of the matter is that neither of us can see jack shit. After a few minutes of blind disorientation, we clumsily feel our way to the stern and ascend to reassess the situation.

Just as we surface, however, I feel my legs being forcefully sucked down and away from the boat. It's not the grip of a creature, though; it's the pull of a powerful undertow. The ensuing drama unfolds quickly and is only partially documented by our cameras. The drag is being generated by the propellers of a behemoth ship that has drifted toward our position, churning the surrounding waters. The current drags both Casey and me along the surface and toward a rusting mooring nearby bobbing violently and threatening to smash our skulls. Despite kicking wildly, we're being pulled underwater and into the tangle of metal and chain that is now listing violently toward our heads. Casey and I choke in the turbulent waters and wave our arms frantically. Our teammates quickly bound up to the highest point of our boat, issuing a flurry of screams to alert the vessel, which promptly shuts down her engines. It's over quickly, and Casey and I are hauled back onto the deck, exhausted and shaken.

This isn't my last brush with catastrophe while making *Destination Truth*. Rather, it's merely the opening act in a cabaret of close calls, all in the name of exploration. I'm not saying that making *D.T.* is dangerous; it's not, per se. It's just that when you go out of your way to find adventure, sometimes adventure tries to bite you on the ass. The key is figuring out how to walk away in one piece.

I'm not talking about survival skills. That's not my domain. If you want to learn how to drink your own pee, eat maggots, and sleep inside animal carcasses, you need to talk to Bear Grylls. Incidentally, a few years ago, Bear took some heat for sleeping in hotels while his show depicted him as roughing it outdoors. Bear and I have never met, but I will say this to his group of small but vocal detractors: When was the last time you received a black belt in karate, survived a free-fall parachute accident, and became the youngest Englishman to summit Everest? Jesus. What's a guy got to do to get a little respect? Oh, and his name is *Bear*. As in, "I'm a bear. I will eat your goddamned face off."

No, my tips for cheating death are entirely more accessible. Little nuggets of advice learned the hard way. In the case of our Vietnamese dive trip, Casey and I would have wound up as fish food in Halong Bay if not for the fast thinking (and loud swearing) help of our colleagues. The incident is a reminder of a lesson best vocalized by the Beatles: *I get by with a little help from my friends.* Never travel with people you aren't willing to depend on. Remember that.

Additional words of wisdom are hereby presented in a series of unfortunate parables.

Machine gun to the face: Senegal

Okay, this was my bad. I drove our crew across the border from Gambia on a bit of crummy advice from a local. I'm a shameless country-counter, and I wanted to get a toe into Senegal so that I could add one more to my irrelevant list of visited nations (yes, a toe counts). I was told that a dirt road off the main highway would lead us to a sleepy Senegalese village with no border patrol whatsoever. Once again: *no border patrol whatsoever.* A few miles later we round a sharp bend to see a group of soldiers jumping to attention. One of them drops down into a foxhole and swings a .50 caliber machine gun toward my head. Another guard quickly loads an AK-47.

Calamities like this resolve in milliseconds; there is no room for trial and error, no second rounds of negotiation. History tells us that the delineation between those who survive disaster and those who do not is very often drawn by one's ability to make sound decisions in the face of acute danger, and do it quickly. You get it right, or you get dead.

1. **Get your bearings.** People frequently report the sensation of time slowing down during moments of disaster. This phenomenon may be caused, in part, by a rapid acceleration of the brain's processing of vital information. Use this momentary heightening of awareness to take a snapshot.

What do you see? In my case: running soldiers. Panicked expressions. Guns. A narrow road.

2. **Fight or flight.** This phrase, coined nearly a century ago, refers to an animal's snap judgment to engage or wuss out when faced with conflict. Make no mistake: running away is usually the right decision at least half the time. Being a dead adventurer is, in my humble opinion, overrated. You can always run away and embellish your bravery later. However, running away under the wrong circumstances can be more disastrous than standing your ground. In this particular instance, the nearly overwhelming instinct to flee would be a terrible mistake. The guards are on the defensive, and trying to evade them would only confirm us as a threat. Also, my ability to turn the car around on this dirt path is no match for a few fully automatic machine guns.

3. **Make a move.** One of the biggest mistakes people make in high-pressure situations is to simply do nothing at all. To freeze. It's important to commit to a decision. In this case, my instincts tell me that the smart money is on defusing the situation as quickly as possible. I stop the car, put my hands in the air to illustrate my utter defenselessness, and smile. Big smile. Smiling helps 90 percent of armed conflicts. Proven fact. So I do my best to stand there like a grinning American idiot (not difficult). Because if there's one thing that people around the world can get behind, it's feeling superior to Americans. Especially people who speak French. Oh, they love it.

We're marched out of the car at gunpoint. I don't speak three words of French, but I manage to understand that these gentlemen would like to see our passports. We produce them slowly and just keep on smiling.

In the end, with the temperature of the situation much cooler, the guards realize that my ragtag pack of monster hunters is a threat to national security; they send us back from whence we came. As I start up the jeep, I point to the ground and ask the guard, "Is this The Gambia or Senegal?"

He looks up with a smirk. "You are in Senegal."

Perfect. Country number seventy-eight.

Lesson: *Make decisions calmly, quickly, and accurately.*

Black hole of death: Chile

Descend into a centuries-old mine to search for an alien entity believed to live in subterranean darkness. You know. Just another Tuesday. In my head, the mine was going to be something I could simply walk into. Maybe a thick-timbered arch and Big Thunder Mountain Railroad tracks leading into a dusky tunnel. Definitely horizontal. Not this. This is the scariest damn thing I've ever seen. A slumping pit in the middle of Chile's Atacama Desert that dates back to the time of the Conquistadores. Various splintered logs and heavy burlap bags are struggling to restrain the sandy embankments, and I can't even get close enough to look down the hole. It's essentially the Sarlacc Pit in *Return of the Jedi* (before Lucas went back and ruined it with that potted plant).

According to a local source, this particular shaft should

be about sixty feet deep, allowing us to rappel down inside and access the maze of tunnels below. When climbing, our policy is to rig redundancy lines for each climber. One line allows an individual to self-descend. A second line is controlled from the top in the event that the climber releases his primary line.

Our director of photography, Evan, and I are going to lead the group. Evan goes first so that he can film me from below. He lowers himself down, using about half the length of his rope, and then yells up for me to begin. I can tell from the timbre of his voice that he's nervous, which is a very bad sign. Evan is a longtime *D.T.* veteran who surfs, climbs, scuba dives, and is generally up for just about any insane activity I throw his way. In all his seasons of making the show, this is the only time I've ever heard genuine fear in his voice. Hooked in, I back toward the rim of the pit and gaze down into a void. Evan is hard to see hanging only fifty feet underneath me. I rappel down about thirty feet. Small rocks hail down and bounce off of Evan's helmet and into the darkness. He calls up at me: "Something's wrong, dude."

I look between my dangling legs and see the flicker of his headlamp below me. "What?" I yell down.

"It's too deep. Listen to the rocks."

I dislodge a small stone from the wall and let it drop from my hand. It sails past Evan and into the nothingness. Silence. The rope creaks. More silence. Evan shines his light down hopelessly. The sound of the rock hitting the bottom is so distant, so small, that it immediately turns my stomach over. This mine shaft is *hundreds* of feet deep.

This is a problem. A big problem. First of all, our ropes are only 100 feet long. What concerns me more is that the rigging at the surface doesn't offer enough leverage to pull us back up. We were planning on resetting the lines from the bottom. Now we're screwed; we have to go back up. I try to use a device called an ascender to hoist myself up the line, but the walls are sheer; there aren't any footholds. I kick off the wall a few times with a grunt before giving up, spinning quietly in the void. Evan and I yell up to the team at the surface that we're stuck. After what feels like an eternity, they call down that they want to hoist Evan up first, since the position of his rigging makes it easier. Great. Inch by inch Evan rises up toward me. Though I can't hear or see what's happening at the surface, I know that the team is digging their heels into the ground in a gravitational tug-of-war. It's laborious and slow work. Eventually, Evan and I are eye to eye. There isn't much to be said. We put our hands on each other's shoulders as he begins to pass upward. "Get me out of here," I whisper.

Night sets in just as Evan clears the top of the shaft. I can no longer tell where the mine ends and the sky begins. I'm in utter and complete blackness. "Josh!" Evan calls down from above. "They need to re-rig your safety line and add some pulleys for leverage. *DO NOT* let go of your other rope."

I watch as the safety line in front of my face goes slack. The only thing keeping me from falling into the abyss is the grip of my right hand. A hand that is sore and turning numb. There's nothing to do but wait.

I shine my light at the wall and notice the faint grooves of chisel marks made by the workers who originally dug this pit of despair. Do you remember that scene in *The Silence of the Lambs* where the senator's daughter is down in that well, and she has to put the lotion in the basket (lest she "get the hose")?

As Buffalo Bill hoists the basket up, the light illuminates fingernail marks on the walls of the well, and she completely and utterly loses her shit. As though before this moment she thought that maybe this situation was going to shake out okay for her. That's me. I see the chisel marks in the wall, feel utterly helpless, and begin to panic. *I'm never getting out of this place. I'm going to die here.*

I turn my headlamp off with my free hand. The darkness is everywhere now. I picture the bottom of the shaft. *How long would the fall take? What would I land on? Skeletons?* Fear begins to unhinge my mind, and I picture alien creatures clinging to the walls or ghoulish miners reaching up at me from the tenebrous depths. The dread moves into my body, paralyzing my muscles. I feel the rope slip an inch through my fingers. I'm very close to tears.

Then I stop. I take a series of deep breaths, lean my forehead against the rope, and tell myself to calm down. I turn the light back on and stare at a groove in the wall, focusing on it with every scrap of concentration that I can muster. I hold fast to my line. In time, the safety rope tightens, and I begin to rise. I let my grip relax and am hoisted toward the surface.

Lesson: *Never, ever panic. It helps nothing and makes the rope slip.*

Hippo attack: West Africa

We decide to take a boat into hippo-infested waters. This turns out to be a bad idea. The lesson here is pretty straightforward: *Leave hippos alone.*

Waterfall of doom: Madagascar

Charging through the cloying, black jungle, I swat at menacing vines and oversized leaves that whip by my face. Madagascar's flora is so otherworldly that I may as well be reenacting a scene from *Avatar*. We've come here looking for a mysterious jungle creature known as the Kalanoro, based on dozens of eyewitness reports generated from this patch of wilderness. Just ahead of me, an animal is getting away, and I want to know what it is. Behind me, our camera operator, Gabe, and sound guy, Mike, are keeping pace. We're running alongside a fast-flowing river.

Suddenly there's nothing ahead of me, and I wave my arms in backward circles to stop my momentum. I slide to a halt at the top of an abrupt cliff. The river plunges over the lip in a spectacular waterfall that cascades down with a roar. I look down into a shimmering lagoon, surrounded on all sides by jungle.

It's an intoxicatingly beautiful place. So much so that I'm drunk with impulsivity. And at that moment, I almost jump. I almost just sail off the edge into the humid night air and the darksome waters below. I don't, though. I feel my muscles relax and the moment pass. "What are you doing?" Mike asks as I squint down at the bottom of the falls.

"Nothing. I was going to jump. I'm not sure how deep it is, though."

"Are you nuts?" Mike asks. "It must be a fifty-foot drop."

"I know, but I think it's deep. Don't you just want to jump off this thing?"

Mike looks over the edge and beams. "Totally." This is the type of people we hire.

The animal we were after is long gone by now. Mike and I hike down to the water's edge to determine the depth of the pool. Gabe stays at the top for a well-earned cigarette. If the water is deep enough, we can scramble back up the ridge and jump.

The hike down is miserable. We slip against crumbling ledges, ensnared by hundreds of plants. At the bottom we draw near to the water's edge, which is choked with vines and spiderwebs. I'm sure there are snakes here, and I'm praying there aren't crocs. Mike and I look at each other in a way that silently conveys: *We're going to take our clothes off now and go swimming in a tropical lagoon together, but it's not going to be weird.*

We strip down, dive into the water, and begin paddling toward the falls. By the time we reach the center of the pool, the sound of the crashing falls is deafening. Still swimming, I look up at the cliff and the cloud-cradled moon beyond. It would almost be romantic if I weren't with a naked Mexican dude. We count to three and submerge. We'd need at least fifteen feet of freeboard here to make the jump viable. Instead, I immediately feel my feet hit the bottom. In fact, I can stand. There are jagged rocks everywhere, and most of the lagoon can't be more than five feet deep.

There is a hardwired function in our minds designed to keep us out of harm's way. Sometimes it's worth overriding that instinct, and sometimes, like tonight, it decidedly isn't. The takeaway here is tried and most certainly true.

Lesson: *Look before you leap.*

Pukefest: Micronesia

I'm sweatier than usual, if that's even possible. Rivulets of water are streaming off my forehead as I walk by torchlight through the jungle ruins. The flickering flame illuminates the basalt walls of an overgrown tomb and the outline of a narrow path beneath my feet. I'm alone and trying to get back to our base camp; I'm not sure that I'm going to make it. A small GPS receiver in my hand illuminates directions for me. But I falter, dropping to my knees, letting the torch be extinguished on the wet ground. I reach into my pocket and grab a headlamp, turning it on with a click and banishing a cone of darkness. Suddenly a thick column of vomit shoots out of my mouth.

Our executive producer, Brad Kuhlman, loves to trot out the Boy Scout motto. Before we leave the country each season, he sits the whole group down and says, "I used to be a Boy Scout, and the Scout's motto is: *Be Prepared.*" I can't help but raise an eyebrow at the fact that while I'm "being prepared," he's back at home golfing, eating sushi, and kicking back in the Hollywood Hills. But that's beside the point.

Back at base camp I am looked over by our paramedic, Shawn, who administers an IV. Over the course of the next few hours, I will vomit eighteen times and receive three bags of much-needed fluid through my arm. I won't even begin to tell you what's happening below my waist. The point is that without the electronics that led me back to camp or the medicines waiting for me there, I might have found myself in an even worse situation.

Now, I'm all for being whisked wherever the wind blows, but when it comes to adventure travel, you need to have the right tools for the job. If you're headed to the ice planet of Hoth, you need to bring a winter coat. If you're hiking across the Sahara, you should carry a canteen or two. And if you're going to muck about in the jungles of the developing world, you need a GPS, headlamp, and access to medicine (in my case, administered by an actual medic).

From pocketknives to granola bars, I hone my travel kit every time I leave the country, learning from my mistakes and adjusting the items I need for the journey at hand. The Boy Scouts (and Brad) are right.

Lesson: *Be Prepared.*

Roof rips off airplane: Romania

The pilot adjusts the flaps and begins to bank around toward an open field. Time seems to slow down, and I think about the circumstances that brought me here. . . . I manage to catch the pilot's gaze for only a moment; above the din he looks at me and yells, "*We must go back!*"

Indeed. We must. With the roof torn off, the aircraft is difficult to control. If the pilot can't land this thing soon, what's left of the plane is going to take a much more direct route to the ground. There's absolutely nothing that I can do to help this situation. I'm powerless, which in itself is the lesson. Sometimes you just can't sway the forces of the universe to better your situation. It's out of your hands from time to time.

Lesson: *Let go and enjoy the ride.*

At the summit
of Mt. Kilimanjaro.
A turning point
in my life.

Blending in while
shooting in Papua
New Guinea.

Making a
new friend
in Malaysia.

The majestic landscape of Tanzania.

A Tanzanian
warrior chanting.

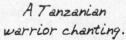

Up close with the
king of the jungle.

A pregnant mother
in Brazilian Amazon.

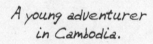

A young adventurer
in Cambodia.

A beautiful
baby in India.

Filming in Kathmandu, Nepal.

Horseback riding at the Pyramids of Giza.

Donating our Bigfoot cast to Joe Rohde and the Yeti Museum at Disney's Animal Kingdom, near Orlando.

Up close and
personal with a
croc in Gambia.

A herd of elephants
cross the Serengeti.

Snuggling
with a snake
in Thailand.

Commuting
on a
helicopter
flight.

A nomadic herder
in Mongolia.

A shave and a
haircut in India.

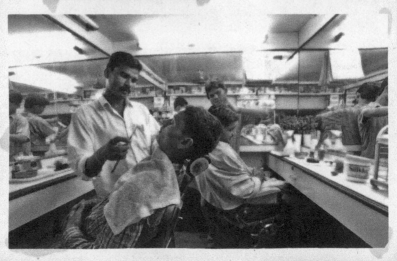

The
foreboding
but beautiful
landscape of
Iceland.

Birds scatter in front
of a mosque in India.

A curious face
in Indonesia.

Anchored
off the coast
of Zanzibar.
It's a rough job,
but someone's
gotta do it.

Ready for the
next adventure!

CASE FILE: *FLYING FIENDS*

NAMES: *Thunderbird, Jersey Devil, Ropen, Kikiyaon, Kongamato, Ahool, Fangalobolo.*

DESCRIPTION: *These are winged predators, commonly reported as large and prehistoric. Other variations include giant bats, oversized owls, or, in the case of the Jersey Devil, an airborne demon.*

LOCATIONS: *British Columbia, Alaska, Africa, Madagascar, Indonesia, Papua New Guinea, and weirdly, New Jersey.*

STATUS: *Evidence of flying cryptids comes almost exclusively from eyewitness reports. Little photographic documentation exists. A common thread is a belief that these creatures live in caves, probably because it answers the troubling question of why we don't regularly see them out in the wild.*

In the age of the dinosaur, massive flying pterosaurs ruled the sky. With a wingspan of up to thirty feet, these long-beaked and leathery-winged predators bear little resemblance to the reptiles of today. But nearly all of these animals share the same modus operandi. They supposedly swoop down from on high, plucking victims off their feet with razor-sharp talons before devouring their unsuspecting lunch. In the case of the Jersey Devil, the beast seems satisfied with just scaring motorists, which, if you've ever driven down the Jersey Turnpike, is actually pretty tough to do.

VERDICT: *After investigating several varieties of flying fiends, I'm happy to go on record as saying that I think the majority of eyewitness recollections are based on actual encounters. Folks who think they've seen an unknown aviator are some of the most earnest I've met. I just think that most of the time they're misidentifying what they're seeing. The major problem is that scale is notoriously difficult to establish in the sky. Without surrounding natural features to provide perspective, estimating an animal's size in flight (not to mention clearly recalling its features) is nearly impossible. In my travels, I've ducked down at the sight of large species of bats with wingspans of four feet. But from the ground they look like that demon in* <u>Fantasia</u>.

Even more problematic is the fact that the regions where stories of these winged behemoths are most prevalent are also home to oversized birds. In 2002 a pilot in Alaska made international headlines when he and his passengers spotted a large, birdlike creature with a wingspan he claimed was the length of his Cessna. Though many believed this to be the legendary Thunderbird of Native American folklore, biologists contend that it might have been a rare Steller's sea eagle, a predatory bird with a nearly ten-foot wingspan.

In a class by itself, tales of the Jersey Devil are some of the richest on record. A bizarrely hoofed, flying biped, the creature has the distinction of being America's oldest monster. Still, the roots of the Devil legend are clearly folkloric (it was rumored to be the satanic offspring of an unlucky local woman), and despite hundreds of years of sightings, there still isn't a shred of physical evidence to support its existence.

As for me, until someone produces a four-foot feather or a bird dropping on my car that's the size of my car, I'm staying on the sidelines. Despite passionate testimony to the contrary and having seen a few anomalies myself, I consider the existence of large flying creatures the least probable of all cryptids.

Take that, Big Bird.

11: Worst. Vacation. Ever.

Cabo San Lucas, 2007

It began, like most disastrous enterprises, innocently enough.
My best friend Jon and I decided to take a road trip. After
spending nearly every waking moment of our summers together
as children, our careers had carried us to opposite coasts. Jon,
a medical student on his way to becoming a doctor, was living
in New York, and I, a burgeoning monster hunter, was in Los
Angeles. Jon had a week off, and I was looking for a little R&R
after a season of *Destination Truth*.

I can't remember which of us decided on Mexico, and for
the sake of our friendship, it's probably better that way. What I
do remember is that we planned for Jon to fly to Los Angeles
and that we'd drive to Cabo San Lucas at the terminal end
of the Baja California Peninsula. What followed remains the
absolute worst trip in a storied career as a professional traveler.
But, like I said, it began innocently enough. . . .

Jon flies to LA, and we spend the night at my loft in
Hollywood before setting off the next morning. Though we
have a full night at our disposal, the extent of our vacation
planning consists of a Google search that reveals the distance
from my front door to Cabo San Lucas as roughly 1,200 miles.

No problem, we think. Should be able to knock that out in a long day.

Day one. We start bright and early, and the drive to the border proves easy enough. The freeway winds down the coast and past the sunny skyline of San Diego. Within three hours we're nearing Mexico. It's around this time that I make the only sensible decision of the entire trip. After hearing horror stories of carjackings, I decide to park on the California side of the border and rent a car on the other side. I call Hertz on my cell phone and get a quote for a rental at the Tijuana airport. The rate is reasonable enough: thirty dollars a day. Mind you, I don't actually book the car. I just check the price.

After parking in an anonymous lot amidst a million other vehicles, we sling backpacks over our shoulders and walk through customs, over the footbridge, and into Mexico. As two gringos crossing the border, we must look appetizing to the horde of loitering locals, who perk up at our approach.

"*Tequila?*"

"*Señoritas?*"

"*Drogas?*"

We wave off their efforts at temptation and head straight for a taxi driver leaning against the hood of his car. "Tijuana airport, *por favor*," I say.

"*Sí, señor.* Forty dollars," he says, opening the door.

"What? The airport is ten minutes from here," I protest.

"Forty dollars, señor."

It takes half an hour of haggling in the morning heat with a dozen different drivers before we get someone to take us to the airport for the lower but still outrageous price of twenty dollars. It's a rocky start.

Inside the terminal, I speed-walk to the Hertz counter, checking my watch and shaking my head. It's already past one in the afternoon, and we're not even out of Tijuana. "Welcome to Hertz, señor. How can I help you?" a fat little man with a gigantic mustache and drooping eyes, inquires.

"*Hola. Necesito* . . . um . . . rent . . . *un auto para seis dias.*"

"Okay. Car for six days. *Sí.* Six hundred dollars," he says.

"What?!" I balk.

Jon turns on his heels, walks away, and sits on a bench behind me. We're clearly going to be here for a while.

"I called the 800 number for Hertz, and I was quoted thirty dollars a day."

He is expressionless. "Is a different number, señor."

"What the hell does that mean? It's the same company."

"Is a different number, señor. Price is six hundred dollars."

"Fine," I exclaim, jamming my credit card and license back into my wallet. "Forget it. I'll rent from another company."

I walk five feet to my right to the Avis car rental counter. The mustached man slides over. "Welcome to Avis, señor. How can I help you?"

I glare at him. I walk on to the Budget counter, and he follows me, step for step. We stop and face each other. "Okay. Look," I say, defeated. "I need a car. I can't pay a hundred dollars a day. You must have something I can rent. A compact?"

He looks at me from under his eyelids and ponders for a moment. Finally he says there's one car available for $400. It's a terrible rip-off, but my cell phone isn't working; I can't get a better quote. Mostly, I really just want to get the hell out of this awful border town. "Fine. Great," I agree.

We're led outside, and another employee brings our car around. Jon and I both pull off our sunglasses to take it in, mouths agape. A VW Beetle (original) with a cheap matte-white paint job. Inside, the car has been burned out and rebuilt. Other than the two aftermarket front seats, there isn't a stitch of upholstery anywhere in the vehicle. Just exposed, rusting metal panels. It's like an ad for tetanus shots. Manual transmission, of course, and no air-conditioning. Intestinal wires spill out of a cavity in the dash where a radio once lived. "It's perfect," Jon says, grinning. And, in a way, it *is* perfect. Other than the rental price, this does seem like an appropriately ridiculous car for such an impromptu south-of-the-border adventure.

Jon jumps in the driver's side; I throw my backpack on what's left of the backseat and slip my sandals off. We're in high spirits as we sputter out of the parking lot, headed to the only slightly less shitty town of Rosarito. It's nearly three in the afternoon.

An hour and a half later, we're sitting in bumper-to-bumper traffic no more than a mile from the airport. We've made little progress, thanks to a Tijuana road construction project that's about as organized as a street riot. Without a radio, we're sitting in silence, Jon with his head against the steering wheel, me with my bare feet hanging out the window. By the time the congestion finally lets up, we're both tired and irritable.

The sun sets somewhere just past Rosarito, and we're both feeling famished. We see a few fires burning on the side of the road, illuminating a makeshift taco stand. We pull over and order up a few plates of grub. It tastes delicious, although it's hard to enjoy on account of the five shady Mexican guys giving us the stink eye from the next table. They're dressed like the gang from *Grease*, and even though my Spanish is elementary, I know enough to understand that they're talking about mugging us. Mexican Danny Zuko smiles at me, and I muster a smile back. We quietly retreat to the car, taking our tacos to go.

The next town looks like it's had a rough couple of centuries, and we check directly into the first motel we see. The room smells like mold, and the only lamp in the room isn't working; at least I can park around back in case the Guacamole Gang from the taco stand drives this way.

In bed, I look over the map by flashlight, working things out in my head. Baja California tears away from the west coast of Mexico like a thousand-mile-long splinter. But the map doesn't tell the whole story. The orderly looking pink line that flows down the paper is, in reality, a writhing two-lane road, unnervingly narrow and badly damaged. It's also clogged with everything from industrial trucks to donkey carts. Our average speed has been maybe forty miles per hour so far. Factoring in these conditions, which I can only assume will get progressively worse, I realize our trip is going to take significantly longer than we anticipated. We're not even a quarter of the way to Cabo.

"Jon, I'm starting to think this might not be the best idea."

"Are you saying you want to quit?" he taunts back from the darkness.

It's exactly what I want to do. "No. I guess not," I say. I click off the flashlight and close my eyes. I have a bad feeling about our predicament and toss and turn all night in the sticky heat.

Day two. Things look better in the morning. Not the town, mind you, but our general confidence. I get behind the wheel cheerily and we set off, bolstered by the promise of a new day.

This lasts about an hour.

By ten a.m. we're about a hundred miles south of the city of Ensenada, and the road, which hugged the Pacific Ocean all morning, has now turned sharply inland, where it will trap us for the remainder of the journey. We are now hemmed in by desert. As the ocean breeze slips away, it is replaced by torturously hot air. Vast, featureless hills of scalding dirt seem to redirect the sun's heat back into our tiny car like a magnifying glass. The temperature climbs to well over a hundred degrees. By noon I've unbuttoned my shirt and am coated with a sheen of sweat; my lips are starting to crack.

The road is awful. Huge swaths of it are unpaved, and our car kicks up torrents of dust as we swerve around potentially fatal potholes and apparently suicidal Mexican children. Our progress is further hampered by an hour-long stop at a gas station, waiting for the attendant to show up. I've had a Dwight Yoakam song stuck in my head all day and hum softly as we sit on the hood of the car, baking in the sun. *I'm a thousand miles from nowhere / Time don't matter to me . . .*

We finally arrive at the border between north and south Baja, where a shotgun-wielding guard at a checkpoint instructs us to shut off the engine. He motions to roll up the windows. I look over as a man in a full hazmat suit wearing an aluminum pesticide backpack from 1938 approaches the vehicle. He looks like the Rocketeer. Jon and I quickly crank up the windows as he starts pumping a lever and spraying the entire car down with a noxious chemical that's either designed to kill insects, Americans, or both. We cough and futilely wave at the air. The guard motions us on. The liquid cooks on the hood of the Beetle, creating a permanent stink inside the car.

Jon takes over driving in the afternoon. Once the sun sets, it becomes intensely dark. There are no arc lights over the road and fewer and fewer towns along the way. My head is resting against the passenger window, and I'm just starting to nod off when I hear Jon whisper, "Shit."

I look up to see red and blue lights reflecting off the dashboard. We're being pulled over. "Stay calm," I say. "Just pull over."

I watch as two police officers armed with machine guns exit the SUV behind us and saunter up to the driver's-side window. "*Buenos noches, señores,*" one of them says. "You make illegal turn."

"We haven't made a turn all night," Jon objects.

It's a shakedown. Plain and simple.

"Step out of the car, señores."

We're asked to stand next to the vehicle, and I gaze out at the infinitely gloomy desert with my arms crossed, trying to guess exactly where we're going to be dismembered and buried.

"You want to go to prison?" the cop asks me.

"No, Officer," I say. "I want to go to Cabo."

"You make illegal turn," he says again.

"We certainly didn't mean to. We don't have much money on us, either," I add meekly. "I'm sorry."

He walks away and talks with his partner.

"What are they saying?" Jon asks.

"Something about money. I think they believe us."

We stand outside for more than half an hour. Eventually the cops realize that we are what we appear to be: two morons with very little cash. They return to their car and simply drive off, leaving us standing alone on the side of the road.

"Let's just find somewhere to sleep," Jon says.

In the next town we come to, houses are in various states of disintegration, and the few roadside restaurants have all been boarded up. There's one hotel sign, and we follow it down a dingy side road. The hotel turns out to be a motel—or at least most of a motel. We drive into the dirt courtyard of a two-floor U-shaped building. The entire right side of the complex has collapsed, taking with it a third of the rooms. Chickens and a goat dawdle out of the way as we pull in and shut off the motor. I get out of the car and promptly set my shoe down into at least two inches of sloppy, wet mud and animal feces. "Son of a bitch," I whisper.

We step up onto the cement porch, wipe our shoes, and follow the fluorescent light of the manager's office to the far end of the building. The door is locked, and I rap on the frame a few times while Jon cups his hands against the glass. Finally, a half-stoned guy whose face is mostly obscured by a scorpion tattoo shuffles in from an adjoining room. He unbolts the door without opening it and just walks over to the desk. We ask for his best room and exchange five dollars for a key.

We head back past about five identical doors to a room situated about twenty feet away from our car. We tiptoe down into the mud and wearily retrieve our bags from the backseat. The only modern convenience on the Beetle is an aftermarket alarm, which I engage before locking the car.

I have to throw my shoulder into our room's metal storm door to get it open. It bursts into what smells like a condemned slaughterhouse, and a few flies desperately escape to freedom. In place of beds are two poured concrete slabs, each with a quarter-inch mattress on top. There are no sheets in sight, just a few ratty pillows, and one pathetic window looks out through metal bars onto a brick wall. I hear a creak and look up at the slowly turning blades of a slumped ceiling fan. Exposed wiring is stapled loosely along the ceiling and leads to a switch by the door.

We throw our bags down. I walk into the bathroom, which seems to be the source of the terrible smell. The mirror above the vanity is smashed into a spiderweb pattern and reflects my face a thousand times. The faucet coughs out chalky water that dumps down through an open hole in the sink and spills onto my feet. The stink of sewage wafts up from the toilet, which is little more than a hole in the corner.

Jon and I don't speak. There isn't much to say. I shut the front door hard and make sure to lock the dead bolt. The heat in here is like a sauna, and we both strip down to our boxers and lay on our cement beds. I swat away another fly and close my eyes until sleep eventually finds me.

I wake sharply to the sound of a shrill electronic cry. *The alarm.* Someone is trying to steal our car. I hustle to my feet, stumbling as I misjudge the height of the bed. Quickly regaining my footing, I grab the door handle and suddenly scream out. A surge of electricity explodes up my arm, and I collapse to the floor. My hand is still clenching the knob as my muscles contract in agony. Jon turns on the lamp and sees that the wiring from the ceiling fan is caught in the frame of the aluminum door. He takes a pillow and swats the wiring out of the jamb, which allows me to retract my arm and get to my feet. Cradling my fried fingers against my chest, I use my good hand to grab my pocketknife from the table and flick out the blade while Jon throws the door open.

As two mostly naked, screaming, barefoot Americans rush headlong into the motel courtyard, three would-be thieves give up on the Beetle and flee around the corner of the building. My feet are under the power of pure adrenaline, and as I leap heroically from the stoop my leg shoots out from under me. I slip like a clown on a banana peel and land on my back in two inches of chicken shit and mud. I lie there groaning, waving a knife haplessly at the moon.

Day three. Dawn. Neither one of us has slept much since the attempted carjacking. I have visible burn marks along each finger, and despite Jon's extensive medical training, the best he can think to do is wrap my hand in a dirty white T-shirt. Both of us stink vaguely of feces and insecticide and drive away from the motel in focused silence. There's no going back now. I'm like Clark Griswold. This is no longer a vacation. It's a mission.

We drive to Cabo as fast as we can, honking past meandering trucks, stopping only when necessary, and pushing the car to its absolute limit. We finally arrive just past noon and head straight for the row of expensive hotels along the coast; I point us toward the most lavish driveway of the bunch. The Beetle comes to a squeaky stop in front of the lobby, pry bar marks along the driver's-side door and caked mud along the once white side panels. The valet looks horrified. "Don't scratch her," I say, throwing him the keys. As we approach the front desk, sunburned and limping, I note a barely disguised look of terror on the front-desk attendant. "I want a room on the water," I announce. "A room that opens onto the beach."

"The charge will—"

"I don't care what it costs," I say, smacking down an American Express card on the marble counter.

The room is as requested. A white-walled suite with blue tile accents and French doors that open right onto the sand. Jon and I tip the bellman and clink together the two flutes of champagne waiting for us on a glass table.

We immediately put on our swim trunks, throw open the doors, and run down the ivory sand toward the indigo-colored surf. The warm, frothy water is like a baptism. We laugh and yell out in relief to have finally made it to Cabo, having prevailed against all the many obstacles of this peninsular gauntlet. I take in a mouthful of water and spit it victoriously in the air. Slipping under, I swim hard against the strong rip current. But just as I surface, a huge wave clocks me right in the face, tumbling me to shore. I pull myself up on the beach, unclogging my ears and adjusting my shorts, which are halfway up my ass. I sit on the sand, half dazed and surprised by the force of the hit. A jewelry seller with an arm full of cheap necklaces strolls behind me. "Big waves, eh?" he says.

"Ya. It's rough as hell out there."

"Big storm coming," he says as he passes by.

"Wait," I call after him. "*What* storm?"

He doesn't look back. "Big storm."

I turn out to sea with new eyes. The surf isn't just rough— it's monstrous. Ominous clouds are gathering above, and I notice for the first time the massive cruise ship that appears to be changing direction offshore. "Oh, no, no, no . . ." I whisper to myself. I run up the beach as fast as I can, leaving Jon in the waves. Heavy rain suddenly erupts out of the sky.

Throwing on a T-shirt, I fly through the lobby and into the business center, where I commandeer the only computer and navigate to CNN.com. The page loads slowly, the telltale rainbow palette of a weather radar map resolving line by line on the front page. I don't bother waiting. The top half of the satellite picture is enough. A massive white spiral bearing down on Baja. We have inadvertently driven straight into the grip of an enormous hurricane.

I catch an American couple at the front desk.

"Do you have an update on the storm?" I ask, looking at the rain coming down in sheets outside.

"It's bad. Category three and gaining, we heard. The airport is closed. The concierge says if you want to get out of town by car, you've got to leave within the next few hours, because the road always washes out."

Back to the beach. Jon is standing in the rain, watching rowboats from the cruise ship come ashore to unload passengers.

"Gatesy . . ."

"I know. We've got to get the hell out of here."

Back in the room, we repack and head for the front desk. We wait at the end of a ten-person-deep queue. I finally sign the receipt, paying $300 for a hotel room that I have occupied for under an hour.

"You drive," I say. "You're better on stick."

We get in the car and peel out of the hotel parking lot like we just robbed the joint. At the bottom of the driveway, Jon slams on the brakes. The city ahead of us is in chaos, and the street is already under nearly a foot of dark brown water. The roads are jammed with fleeing tourists, boats on trailers, and thousands of people trying to get away from the coast. Jon grips the shifter and swerves out into the fray. I look up at the hillside to see rivers of water pouring down into the streets, and raw sewage bubbles up from the drains.

Jon puts two wheels on the sidewalk to avoid a boat trailer and then drops back down onto the street. "Turn!" I call out, spotting a side street, but it's too late. The main road dips down, and the water level rises halfway up the car. Chocolate water pours in through the doors, bringing with it an unimaginable stench. Our feet are well underwater by the time we shift gears and speed up an alley to higher ground. I can't believe the car is still running. We link up with the main highway and drive north until the rain tapers out. Hurricanes may be dangerous as hell, but one thing they're not is particularly fast. Within an hour the rain relents, and the black clouds are well behind us.

At a gas station I pay four guys to help us tilt the Beetle on its side and drain the water out onto the sidewalk. We use a hose to spray out the interior, but it's a lost cause. The car is saturated with sewage and will never smell right again. I actually miss the insecticide.

I start the engine up and peel out onto the road. The plan from this point on is never discussed; it's simply understood: we're going home. Other than refueling, we don't stop at all. When one of us gets tired, the other silently takes over, driving the 1,200 miles straight on through the night.

Day four. Twenty hours later we arrive in Tijuana, return the car, catch a cab to the border, and walk back across the bridge. A customs agent stamps my soggy passport and hands it back to me with a knowing wink. "Welcome home, boys."

The stomachaches and diarrhea arrive in waves by the time we get to Los Angeles, and both of us have fleas that take a week to kill.

Our trip to Mexico was nothing short of a living nightmare. Jon and I don't talk about it very often, not unless we've had enough to drink to bear the memory. Despite my insistence that improvised travel is one of the most rewarding ways to see the world, it sometimes goes tits up in a truly spectacular way. But then again, that awful week provided me with a great story, a killer wedding toast, and a chapter in my book. So maybe not a total loss after all.

12: Threes and the Christmas Miracle of Whore-Dice

Friendly competitions of strategy and chance have been around since man first learned how to whittle crude game pieces. Variants of checkers are more than one thousand years old. Mancala, even older than that. In present-day Iran, archaeologists unearthed a five-thousand-year-old backgammon game and the oldest dice ever discovered.

A history of games is a history of fraternity. Games are the inspiration for many of our most important bonding moments and a lightning rod for our most arbitrary fights (I'm sure caveman game night never ended well). In my childhood, we played factory-made favorites like Monopoly, Scrabble, and Trivial Pursuit. Today, video games are quickly supplanting the classics, but no matter the platform, be it a wooden board or a Play Station 3, games are still a prominent feature of our upbringing. A familiar touchstone that brings us together. They're home.

Which is why, thousands of miles away, we play them on *Destination Truth*. Also, we like to gamble. A lot. Since nearly the beginning of the show, the crew and I have been playing something called Threes. It is, in my humble opinion, a nearly perfect travel game, and in just about any scene on *D.T.*, there's usually a small pouch of dice tucked in my back pocket. I reproduce the rules here for anyone bound for ports unknown. If you aren't interested in such things or are morally opposed to betting on games of chance, feel free to skip to the next chapter. Actually, feel free to skip to wherever you like. You really don't need me telling you how to read a book.

I've read that the game is also called Tripps, but the origin is completely unknown to me. It came to *Destination Truth* courtesy of our second-season audio guy, Ponch, who had picked it up from the crew on *Survivor*. Where they learned it, I have no idea.

Threes requires five dice and a flat surface. That's it. Hell, even the flat surface is negotiable. We once played on the lurching deck of a fishing boat.

The rules are simple. Every side of each dice is worth its face value, except for the three side, which is worth zero. The point of the game is to get the lowest score. The player rolls all five dice. Then, leaving *at least* one die (if there are any threes showing, the player would obviously want to leave those), the player collects the remainder and recasts. Once the player is out of rolls (if he leaves only one dice down after each throw, he could throw a maximum of five times), he adds the values of the dice to calculate his final score. A perfect round would end with five threes (and zero points).

Play then passes to the left until everyone has a turn. The player with the lowest score wins the pot. The winner rolls last in the next round (the person sitting to his left goes first).

A few important side rules:

1. **One round of Threes costs the equivalent of one dollar in any currency.** The use of obscure money (including shells or livestock) is encouraged. Lying about the conversion rate of foreign currency is also encouraged, if you can get away with it.

2. **The game is best enjoyed while consuming copious amounts of a locally produced alcoholic beverage.**

3. **No touching dice that you intend to keep in play.** You touch it, you reroll it. Arguments will ensue on this point.

4. **No sloppy dice.** If, in the process of collecting or shaking the dice in your hands, one or more of them gets dropped, those dice are not allowed to be rerolled. You're stuck with them. Arguments will also ensue on this point.

5. **Do not interrupt dice on their journey.** If a dice goes skittering off the table, let it go. If it plops into the ocean, it's still fair game. You just have to find it.

A word of warning. Novice players invariably attempt to change Rule #1 once they've strictly adhered to Rule #2. I'd like to warn against the drunken raising of stakes. I participated in a hastily conceived $100 per round game one night in Cambodia. Have you ever seen *Casino Royale*? It ended pretty much the same way.

My team and I have a layover and are drinking our way through an always dangerous one night in Bangkok. Considering our long-standing interest in dice games, I am naturally transfixed by the sight of a chain-smoking prostitute rolling dice in a wooden box. We had just wandered into Nana Plaza, a broad, horseshoe-shaped alley that just might have more illegal things going on per square foot than any other place on earth. With the dubious distinction of being the world's largest sex complex, it looks like a scene out of *Blade Runner*. I half expect a replicant to come crashing through the plate-glass windows.

On the decaying balconies above, prostitutes lean over the railings, unsuccessfully beckoning my team and me to the upper levels. The woman with the dice game is sitting alone at a long table on the ground floor. Fascinated, I grab a couple of Tiger beers and pull up a chair. After politely declining a hand job, I offer her a beer instead; she shrugs and agrees to teach me the rules.

The contraption turns out to be simple enough. The weathered box is maybe one foot by one foot long. Wooden tiles along the top can be flipped up. The tiles are numbered one through seven. Along their underside are seven letters that spell out the word "J-A-C-K-P-O-T." Each time the player rolls the two die, the value of one dice or the other or both can be used to flip a tile (dice showing a two and three could be used to flip either the two, three, or five tile). If you manage to flip all tiles before an unusable roll, you win. It's not easy to defeat, but it is quite fun. Before I know it, the rest of the crew is crowded around, and we've attracted a swarm of locals. In what passes for a cultural exchange program, we teach the prostitutes how to play Threes, and they teach us the box game. I ask what it's called, and one of the coquettish girls flashes a wink and purrs, "Whore-Dice."

"I want one of these," I announce. "Where can I buy one?"

"Now?" the woman asks. "It's one a.m."

"Yeah. How much?"

"Five dollars," she says. "But not now. Store closed."

"We'll give you twenty dollars per set," I tell her, "but we need them now. We won't be here tomorrow."

She takes off like a shot. I don't know who she wakes up or what store she breaks into, but within ten minutes she's back with an armload of boxes. We each happily overpay and spend the wee hours of the morning laughing and shooting dice under a neon moon.

After we finish filming the season, I fly home to my parents' house in Boston. It's Christmas Eve. As I'm unpacking my bag in my old room, I take out the aged box and place it on my bed. My father looks over and exclaims, "Shut the Box!"

"What?"

"Shut the Box," he says.

"You mean 'Whore-Dice'?"

"What?"

"It's called Whore-Dice," I say matter-of-factly.

"It's called Shut the Box, son. What do whores have to do with this?"

At the precise moment as I was innocently cavorting with sex workers in Bangkok, my parents were visiting our relatives in New Mexico. While there, one of my cousins introduced my father to a game, which, though it had been dressed up a little for resale, was exactly the same as the one I encountered in Thailand. It was labeled Shut the Box. Turns out it's also called Batten Down the Hatches, Tric-Trac, and High Rollers. Also, Whore-Dice, apparently. References to the game exist as far back as the twelfth century, and it spread to the far corners of the world by sailors, among whom it was intensely popular. It makes sense that it eventually came to Bangkok, since sailors and prostitutes go together like . . . sailors and prostitutes.

So there we sat, that Christmas Eve. Mom warmed up some of her famous New England clam chowder, Dad sank down in his big Dad chair, and the three of us sat laughing by the crackling fire, playing Shut the Box while a light snow began to fall.

Thank you, Thai prostitutes. You made my Christmas.

13: Yeti

Kathmandu is a city that doesn't want to be found, obscured within the vast, undulating valleys that fringe the bottom of the tallest and least accessible peaks on earth: the Himalayas. It's all but impossible not to press one's face against the airplane windows during the final approach, which incites awe in even the most jaded of frequent flyers. The capital appears, glinting in the morning sunlight on an improbable mountain plateau, unfolding in a patchwork of winding streets and dilapidated temples. It's a high-altitude mash-up of religions, architecture, and ethnicities nestled more than a mile above sea level. This city has also been the unlikely birthplace of lavish kingdoms and soaring artistic achievements. This is a traveler's city, the kind of exotic destination that raises your pulse without even trying. And even though I don't have a clue what Bob Seger is on about in that song of his, one thing's for sure: he *really* wants to get to Kathmandu.

We've come here to launch an expedition with the goal of finding evidence of the yeti, one of the heavy hitters in the Cryptozoological Hall of Fame. Truth be told, the yeti is actually my all-time favorite monster. Sightings of this elusive primate date back to time immemorial, and despite little physical evidence to support his existence, the sheer volume and historic legacy of eyewitness reports are endlessly compelling. Modern reports started circulating in 1921, when British Army explorers returned from a reconnaissance mission to Everest. They brought back tales of a mysterious creature well known to the Himalayan people. Soon after, a newspaper coined the moniker "Abominable Snowman," and the West's fascination with the yeti was born. Even Sir Edmund Hillary claimed to see mysterious footprints on his record-setting Everest bid in 1953.

Over the years, the creature blossomed into a cryptid celebrity, pursued by dozens of explorers chasing after him like paparazzi. Though it is head-scratching that a monster thought to rip people limb from limb would be marketed to children, the A-list beast was famously featured in Hergé's *Tintin in Tibet*. Also, in what has to be one of the most surreal television sequences ever conceived, the yeti's teeth are unceremoniously ripped out of his mouth by an elf with a pair of pliers in the animated classic *Rudolph the Red-Nosed Reindeer*. Perfect for the wee ones. Today, his fortunes seem to have waned, forcing him to appear in the Syfy Channel movie *Yeti: Curse of the Snow Demon* and to cameo alongside Brendan Fraser in the blisteringly awful *Mummy: Tomb of the Dragon Emperor* (a movie also notable for not actually featuring a single mummy).

There are an array of theories about what exactly eyewitnesses are seeing in the Himalayas, with many experts writing off the yeti as a misidentified brown bear or nothing more than the bastard offspring of folklore and superstition. The fact of the matter, though, is that people in disconnected villages

scattered throughout the Himalayas have issued strikingly
consistent descriptions of the same creature for thousands of
years. From Tibet to Nepal to Bhutan, the details vary only
slightly, and the through line is the same: the Snowman is real.

Before arriving, the team and I pore over as many of these
accounts as we can, many emanating from remote mountain
towns. One thing's for sure: looking for a yeti in the Himalayas
is certainly going to be an enormous pain in the ass. This is one
of the most extreme environments on earth, and moving an
expedition through these mountains takes Herculean effort.

We check into the famed Hotel Yak & Yeti, an institution
in Kathmandu. Considering its reputation, the rooms are
surprisingly plain, and the entire establishment could use a
little freshening up. However, the staff are hospitable and the
location unbeatable. Once we settle in, I hit the streets, where
I happily find myself lost in the endless maze of Thamel. I
stroll past stores crammed with knockoff North Face gear
(North Fake, as it's known locally), pashmina scarves, and
glittering gemstones. Narrow lanes deposit me into expansive
courtyards framed around pyramidal temples and the high
red walls of the former royal palace. I slowly gawk through the
squares, and it isn't long before a young boy latches onto me,
asking for money. I tell him that I'm staying at the Yak & Yeti,
and if he can find me five good dice by sunset, I'll give him
something for his trouble. He sprints away, calling back to me
in broken English that he won't let me down. I wander with
abandon, photographing as I go. The sun slips below the palace
walls, casting an evening shade onto the cobblestone streets.
The sights and smells of Kathmandu are powerful narcotics,
dizzying my thoughts and drawing me along.

Eventually, I'm so turned around that I have to hail a rickshaw to take me back to the hotel. A tattered photo of the driver's family is taped to the inside of the bonnet. I suddenly remember that it's Thanksgiving, and I smile at the annual memory of my mother shooing me out of the kitchen while I steal a few bites of her delicious cooking.

The rickshaw comes to a stop, and I step down to see the young boy skulking in the alley near the Yak & Yeti, probably fearing the consequences of venturing onto hotel property. He's managed to scrape together a miserable assortment of plastic dice of varying colors and sizes. Though they aren't at all what I wanted, he's clearly done his best. I give him a big thumbs-up and fork over a few hundred rupees, to his delight.

I regroup with the team, and we head to a local rooftop restaurant that is serving, beyond all odds, turkey and all the fixings. The enterprising owner caters to the American ex-pat community in the city and had the birds flown in all the way from Australia. The dinner may not be quite like Mom makes it, but nobody's complaining. The food and the company are satisfying and warm, and there's much to be thankful for. I momentarily tune out the merry conversation and gaze out at the silhouette of an ornate pagoda rising up in the twilight. It's a privilege to be here, eating in the company of this graceful old city. I soak in as much of the night as I can, mindful that tomorrow will arrive too soon, with much work to be done.

Before we leave Kathmandu, we interview a variety of primatologists and local experts who help to narrow our search by zeroing in on a "Goldilocks" zone. At too low an altitude, the locals who populate the mountain slopes would surely spot the animal regularly. At too high an altitude, a large primate would struggle to find sustenance and shelter. In order for the yeti to both stay off the radar and find sustenance, the habitat has to be, like the fairy tale says, juuuust right. The experts suggest an altitude between 9,000 and 15,000 feet. We cross-reference that band of elevation with eyewitness reports and soon found ourselves plotting a course into the Annapurna region. Annapurna is Sanskrit for "full of food," which, though it sounds promising, belies the fact that it contains some of the most barren and hostile mountains on earth.

In order to penetrate the Himalayas, we have to catch a flight to the high mountain town of Lukla. From there, we plan to trek toward Everest base camp, stopping at various eyewitness locations along the way. We also hope to examine a legendary yeti scalp in the Buddhist monastery in Khumjung. This is one of a number of isolated monasteries that claim to house venerated yeti remains in shrines. The most famous is perhaps the Pangboche monastery, which once displayed a severed yeti hand. But in 1959 a member of a yeti expedition stole a section of the hand and had it sent illegally back to the United States under the watchful eye of the most unlikely smuggler in history: Jimmy Stewart. The remains made it to America, where they were deemed inconclusive. The rest of the hand was stolen in the 1990s and is probably now sitting in the private collection of some real-life Dr. No.

We arrive at the tiny domestic air terminal just before dawn. An army of trekkers and Sherpas are jammed up against every counter, trying to get themselves and all manner of climbing gear onto various flights. There isn't an airline here that I've heard of, and I gaze up quizzically at signs for Cosmic

Air and Buddha Air, names that are decidedly at odds with the frustrated, swearing passengers below.

Our airline, the appropriately named Yeti Air, manages a small fleet of decaying Twin Otter aircraft that entered service more than thirty years ago and have been on active duty every day since then. We eventually shove our way through security (I get through with a pocketknife and lighter, if that's any indication of the crack team working here) and slip out onto the tarmac, only to find that a layer of fog has rolled in and delayed our departure. We stroll the runway, taking in the eerie sunrise and thick vapor enveloping the tattered planes parked along the airstrip. After a while, I hear a propeller jump to life far behind me and turn back to see the flight crew waving us into the cabin.

The flight takes only about thirty-five minutes, but it's memorable. Along with seats for about fifteen people, our plane is crammed with equipment, fuel canisters, lumber, and just about anything else the pilot can jam into the cabin. The aircraft door rattles, exposed wiring hangs down above me, and the sound of the obsolescent engines is deafening. The lone flight attendant has wedged herself on top of a wooden crate, her head bent to one side and pressed against the ceiling. The extent of the in-flight service is a bowl of hard candies, which she has us pass amongst ourselves.

The indescribable view of the planet's most magnificent peaks helps distract me from the nearly omnipresent signs that the plane is on the verge of disassembling mid-flight. The mountains rise up quickly on all sides, and the rooftops of Kathmandu quickly recede, giving way to lonely villages and simple farms. The plane creaks and buffets in the strong, cold wind, and visibility turns to nothing (which is just what you want when slaloming through the highest mountain passes in the world). Finally, we drop down through the clouds and bank hard toward a cramped little town poised on the edge of a cliff.

The Lukla airstrip is an absolute horror to behold. Short, narrow, and tilted at an improbable fifteen-degree angle, it begins at a precipice and ends with a high stone wall a scant 1,500 feet away. The pilot makes a flurry of last-minute adjustments to the controls and slams the plane down onto the runway, rapidly braking before we reach the dead end. It's a rush, and everyone on board (including the squished flight attendant) seems thrilled to be in one piece. Six months from now this same plane will miss the runway altogether, killing all eighteen people on board.

Lukla is like a strange refugee camp, with barbed wire surrounding the airstrip. A crush of Sherpas unloads cargo and food, hauling it up and away from the airport. The morning air is freezing, since the sun hasn't yet breached the towering range; I can see my breath as I step down from the plane. We shuffle past a few army officers, walk through the fences, and enter what passes for a town. The cobblestone streets are slick with water, yaks commingle with the local vendors, and there seems to be animal feces almost everywhere. Nearly every building is littered with signs advertising lodging and food, while tiny shops hawk backpacks, climbing gear, and last-minute supplies for teams departing for Everest base camp. It feels kinetic here as we make our way through the fray and toward the trail.

The hike from Lukla to the next village, Phakding, is short—only a few hours, and most of it is at a surprisingly even grade. The scenery cannot be justly described but appears to be hijacked from an alpinist's dream. I'd be amazed if there's a prettier hike in the world. Snowcapped peaks sail above picture-perfect rows of pine trees. The trail hugs both sides of an emerald green river, and we cross over countless narrow footbridges that span the torrent below. Every few hundred meters we're delighted to encounter a faded rainbow of fluttering Buddhist prayer flags and script-carved rocks. It's like trekking through a Tolkien novel, and if a bearded wizard passed us on the trail, I wouldn't bat an eye. By early afternoon the sun is shining high in the sky, and we cross a small suspension bridge into Phakding, which is little more than a cluster of houses strewn along the bank of the river. We set down our heavy packs and warm up with lemon tea and biscuits before settling in for a late-afternoon schedule of not doing a damned thing. At this altitude, we're more than happy for a chance to rest. The sunset, while beautiful, is accompanied by a terrible chill in the air, and we soon retreat to our rough-looking accommodations.

Daylight. I slowly come to life in the cocoon of my sleeping bag, and it takes me a few minutes to process just how freezing I am. I push my head up through the opening and into the blinding light of this makeshift bedroom. I'm on the second floor of what the Nepalese call a "teahouse." I call it a frigging meat locker. The building has no heat, and the thin plyboard walls do little by way of insulation. The two windows are without curtains, and since neither one will latch, cold air is leaking in all around me. A bare lightbulb on a wire swings above in the breeze. I'm sleeping in most of my clothes, so getting dressed only involves slipping into my hiking boots, which is at least convenient, I suppose.

I make my way outside, where it's colder, if that's even

possible. I rush along the cobbled path, teeth chattering, to the dining room, which I'm hoping has a hot stove. I stumble through the door to find most of our porters and Sherpas huddled around in a circle, gambling. In retrospect, maybe we shouldn't have taught them how to shoot dice and play Threes. I throw a few rupees into the pot and rattle the freezing dice in my hands. A cherubic young Nepalese girl hands me a mug of milk-tea, a piping hot combination of black tea, yak milk, and butter. It's an acquired taste but fills me up quickly, banishing the cold. I lose my money to one of the Sherpas, which makes them all squeal with delight. Before long, the rest of the crew arrives, and we look over the contours of the trail map while devouring plates of fried eggs. After breakfast, we say good-bye to our generous hosts. The sun is now over the ridge and warming up the trail as we walk uphill toward a cerulean blue sky.

The hike starts off gentle but quickly turns steep, causing our group to schism into two packs. I struggle to stay in the lead group with Dawa, our main Sherpa. Our camera operator, Erica, who hails from Jackson Hole, Wyoming, flat-out runs up the hill. And surprisingly, our audio guy, Ponch, who isn't exactly a picture of health, is in the lead as well. Brad, Casey, T-Bone, and Araceli filter toward the back, huffing in the thin air. At one point, during a break, Brad tries to stand up too quickly and nearly topples over.

Suddenly, at the top of a high ridge, we all stop in our tracks. Everest. Its rocky peak sits heavy and silent, lording over an impossibly endless range of mountainous subjects. We stand around in reverent silence as though we've suddenly been granted an audience with Vito Corleone. Here, amidst such epic peaks and troughs, the yeti seems a plausible resident.

By the time we reach the village of Namche, everyone is pretty well gassed. Brad, Araceli, and T-Bone look like they might actually drop. Despite our collective exhaustion, the beauty of Namche is hard to ignore. It's a horseshoe-shaped trading post on an 11,000-foot hill surrounded by 20,000-foot peaks on either side. In the center of the enclave is a sprawling bazaar where Nepalese traders offer lovingly made crafts and clothes to anyone hearty enough to make the journey. Merchants from Tibet trek for over a week through treacherous passes to reach the market. It's a serene melting pot of cultures, and we drift through the emporium like a breeze. We eventually land on the icy steps of our lodge, where thin-looking walls promise even colder accommodations than the night before—although I'm encouraged by the sight of some sort of water heater in my makeshift bathroom.

After checking in, we interview locals who live on the outskirts of Namche, listening intently to their stories of the yeti while cozily sipping tea. The accounts vary only slightly, with most residents claiming to have seen the yeti's handiwork (downed trees, mauled livestock) rather than the beast itself. Those who do claim to have spied the Snowman with their own eyes offer tantalizing descriptions of a massive bipedal primate that stands more than eight feet tall. The stories rouse my imagination, and on our way back to the lodge I find myself anxiously hurrying along the dark trail, glancing over my shoulder as I go.

Morning again. It hits me like a brick to the face, and I'm shaking so badly from the cold that I can hardly see straight. I rush to the bathroom, where I crank the hot water on full blast in both the primitive shower and sink, causing clouds of steam to fill the entire room. Soon it's misty and warm, and I can hardly see. I imagine that I'm in the Amazon, my fantasy broken only by the snow-covered vista outside my window. At breakfast I keep my head down and innocently sip my tea as the rest of the crew bitches about the lack of hot water in the complex. Whoops.

We hike on for a few hours to the tidy village of Khumjung, tucked in a valley. The lack of wind here makes the temperature feel a bit warmer, and people mill about in the bright sunshine. As we stroll into town, children run past us and into the dusty field of the Khumjung School, founded by Sir Edmund Hillary.

We approach the Khumjung monastery to view the rumored yeti remains. I've been assured by my contacts back in Kathmandu that I won't have any problem filming here, which is why I'm more than a little surprised to see an elderly monk burst through the doors and hurl a rock at my face. So much for the virtues of peace. Luckily, Buddhist monks throw like little girls, and I'm able to dodge the projectile. The residents of the monastery are, in fact, quite sensitive to outsiders, and it takes an hour of discussion to reach détente and broker a friendly arrangement that allows us inside.

Long after sunset, we're welcomed in to examine the remains. The interior of the temple is dark and empty. The walls are painted with colorful but peeling pigments, and a central Buddha statue majestically overlooks the scene. We're led to a rather unceremonious metal cabinet, which the monk unlocks and opens. Inside is a glass case containing a large brown scalp. Even though I'm skeptical about its authenticity, I have to admit, it looks really convincing. We want a sample—a single hair for DNA analysis. The monk is resolutely opposed. He explains that, years ago, the monks gave strands of the hair to curious trekkers who traveled to the monastery, and as a result, the scalp grew patchy, a baldness brought on by decades of follicular deforestation. Realizing that their generosity was destroying the precious artifact, they now seek to preserve the scalp for the next generation. The monk gives us an earnest look. "If we continue to give away hairs, soon there would be no hairs to give." He's like a cross between Yoda and a fortune cookie, and it's tough to argue with him.

Brad presses him for the sample, though, noting that if the hair fibers yield results, it would prove the scalp is real. "The scalp *is* real," the monk counters. "We can see it. We can touch it. That is enough. We need no validation." It's a sobering point of view. Our Western propensity for cynicism and mistrust is of little interest here. At these heights, fact and belief are merged together, and truth is something to be attained, not challenged, the quest for empirical evidence supplanted by the quest for enlightenment.

With the remains at Pangboche stolen and the scalp at Khumjung safely locked away, we're going to have to find our own specimen. Having reached the altitude band where the creature would most likely live, we set out at dusk to cover as much ground as possible. Even though our array of night-vision equipment allows us to see across huge distances, the terrain here is challenging and slows us down considerably. We scour the forests, slipping down embankments and crossing icy streams before cautiously exploring a set of caves

(yetis may or may not be real, but bears sure as shit are).
Our efforts prove fruitless, and by dawn we're exhausted and
turning to Popsicles.

After another day of hiking and searching, it's beginning
to feel like we're looking for that proverbial needle. Since
everyone is licked, we decide to let some of the team stay back
and keep warm by a stove in the village. After shoveling down
a few bowls of hot soup, a skeleton crew comprised of myself,
Araceli, Erica, Ponch, and a few Sherpa escorts sets out for
another night investigation. We happen upon a tributary of the
large river that bisects this valley and dedicate the beginning
of our search to the forested side of the stream. Other than
hearing a few twigs snap in the darkness, we don't come up
with much. We cross the water to the rockier side of the bank.
I peer through the darkness but don't see anything of interest.
Hell, I can barely see the members of my own team. As I shine
my flashlight under a few huge boulders, I hear one of our
Sherpas excitedly call out, "Josh, Josh!"

I spin around, my eyes focusing on his headlamp a
few hundred feet behind me. By the time I get to him,
he's crouching down, shining his light on the ground. I'm
speechless. More specifically, I'm in shock.

I radio to Brad, Casey, and the rest of the team back at the
village, my voice shaking as I yell out instructions. "Grab the
casting powder! We found a giant footprint!"

The print is about seventeen inches long, with five digits
and a generally anthropomorphic shape. Also, there's a partial
second footprint in front of the first, which is intersected by a
rock, preserving only the back half of the foot. In addition, a
poorly preserved print sits behind both of these, in the softer

sand. My mind is racing, trying to explain away these gigantic impressions.

The rest of the team arrives and races down the embankment to our position. I direct their eyes along the ground with my flashlight beam, shining it onto the prints. Everyone is agape. "Are you kidding me?!" Brad exclaims.

We're now at a fever pitch of excitement. Our Sherpa is beside himself, and the team immediately erupts in discussion over the print. The investigation turns into an excavation; we spread out case after case of gear on the nearby rocks and erect light panels around the site.

The process of casting and extracting both the full and partial prints takes some time but goes smoothly. My discovery in Malaysia has provided me with some experience in this arena, after all. While the plaster is hardening, the team scours the rest of the ridge for additional prints, hair samples, feces, or material remains, but we find nothing. Carefully, we deliver the castings to our camp where we get warm and get fed.

In the morning, we determine that hiking the prints back down to Lukla is too risky. After all, this is what we came for, and one fall could shatter our evidence into a million pieces. We fire up the satellite phone and call in a chopper to shuttle us down to the airstrip. The helicopter arrives, and we wave the pilot onto the ridge. With no helipad here, he simply sets down in a cabbage patch, allowing us to pile in. As we lift off, the pilot dons an oxygen mask and takes us up to over 17,000 feet. My head spins in the thin air, and we bank down along the river toward lower altitudes.

We have to wait until morning for the next flight out of Lukla, so we do the only sensible thing and celebrate in a village bar. Countless bottles of Everest brand beer are cracked open, and we shoot dice on a tattered pool table and drunkenly sing along to Dire Straits and CCR, which blasts through an old stereo. In the corner, a crudely wrapped package conceals a set of yeti footprints. It's a hell of a party that goes until the wee hours of the night. Finally, the crew begins to peel off, weaving through the cobblestone streets to a nearby lodge. Following behind, Brad and I stagger into the now opaque evening, wisely entrusting the prints to a sober Sherpa just before the two of us fall into a gutter.

At first light, we all trudge over to the airstrip and sit on the tarmac, waiting for the plane's arrival. We're all brutally hungover; Erica gets up at one point and literally barfs *on* the runway, which is sort of impressive. We meet the plane and wait to board while about ten cases of Everest beer are offloaded, pleased with ourselves at the inventory that needs to be replenished. As we climb up the aircraft's stairs, the Yeti Air footprint logo on the tail of our plane catches my eye; a fat grin erupts on my face.

The plane lands, and a car brings us to the Hotel Yak & Yeti, where journalists have gathered. It seems the news of our discovery has traveled on the coconut wire down to the capital. Cameras snap furiously as we're ushered into a conference room for an impromptu press conference. I even notice reporters from Al Jazeera and Reuters. We answer questions, produce the prints, and spend the afternoon conducting interviews for international media outlets. It's surreal.

By the next morning we're on the cover of every paper in Nepal, and CBS and CNN have both run stories on us in the States. I'm woefully misquoted in a local newspaper as saying,

"The Snowman is no longer legend for us," a statement that makes me sound like a total nut job. I celebrate my newfound celebrity status by treating myself to a cheap haircut at the hands of an old Indian barber who also trims my eyebrows and throws in a neck massage. Not bad for three bucks.

In the evening we proceed to the famous Rum Doodle restaurant, an obligatory stop for those climbing Everest. A long-standing tradition here demands that teams sign their names on paper cutouts shaped like yeti prints, which are then pinned to the walls. Every square inch of the restaurant is covered in footprints, memorializing thousands of climbers, including the members of the famed Krakauer expedition chronicled in *Into Thin Air*. We're quickly recognized from all the press coverage and are invited to add our names to the venerated walls. If any of you are in Kathmandu, you can find our signatures fastened to the ceiling above the bar.

Back in the States, the castings are subject to a battery of analysis. We take them to Dr. Jeffrey Meldrum of Idaho State University, a respected professor of anatomy and anthropology. He's also a renowned footprint specialist and manages a collection of more than two hundred mystery primate impressions. Meldrum digitizes our evidence using a three-dimensional laser scanner. The results are intriguing. Based on the size and contour of the two prints, the computer confirms a match. In other words, they are anatomically consistent and, considering the depth of the impression, suggest a 300- to 400-pound culprit.

I've been asked a lot whether I think the footprints could have been manufactured. The short answer is: yes. Anything is possible. Having said that, I think it's very unlikely. After all, we were hiking through extreme and remote wilderness on an improvised route known to no one, not even ourselves. We were wandering. Also, the prints are matching, which means that someone would have had to be carrying two detailed molds or models, possess intimate knowledge of primate anatomy, and accurately calculate stride and weight. So. Pretty doubtful. At no point during my trip did someone say, "Oh, have you met Dawa? He's a Sherpa now, but he was a special-effects artist on *Planet of the Apes*. He lives right over there by that river."

However, I can't say to a surety that a yeti is responsible for the prints, either. To me, they look a bit, well . . . goofy. The bulbous, splayed toes and immense size make me want to smile more than recoil in terror.

Though the analysis of the find is extremely compelling, it's also finite. There's only so much information that can be gleaned from a footprint, and once the data has been collected, we're left to figure out what to do with our plaster souvenir. The print makes its way back to our production office, where it sits patiently on a desk between Brad and me. "What are we going to do with this thing, Gates?" Brad asks. The answer presents itself six months later in Orlando.

To my parents' dismay, I was born a Disney enthusiast. When I was a kid, we would go to Florida annually, at my insistence. Every February or April vacation, my poor mother and father would be reluctantly pulled through the turnstiles of Walt Disney World, suffer the indignity of endless cycles on It's a Small World, and endure a few hundred voyages with the Pirates of the Caribbean. When I turned sixteen, my mother finally snapped. Mentally strained from years of helplessly looking on as

- -

animatronic buccaneers raped and pillaged that poor Caribbean town, she'd finally had enough. "No more!" she defiantly announced in her proper British accent. "I can't take those bloody pirates anymore." Before I could protest, she leveled a finger at me and decreed, "We're not going back there until you give me a grandchild." Well played, Mom. Well played.

My parents now spend four months of the year in Florida (in Sarasota, at a generous distance from Disney World). In the span of two years they've gone from hearty New Englanders to self-described "snowbirds." Suddenly they eat dinner at 4:45 in the afternoon, play bocce, and drink Moxie soda.

My girlfriend and I have flown down to visit them. At six thirty one evening, we're already back at their condo after dinner at the Outback Steakhouse, a restaurant that my mother is now referring to as "incredible." Their nightly après-meal ritual involves my father watching television and yelling at Alex Trebek while my mother clips coupons for Subway sandwiches out of the Pelican Press. I remind her that the foot-long subs are literally five dollars to begin with. She just shakes her head and keeps on clipping. On the TV, Alex is squinting at the Double Jeopardy board, which sends my father round the bend. "Jesus. Put your glasses on, Trebek!" my father blurts out.

The next morning my girlfriend and I excuse ourselves from the breakneck pace of life in Sarasota and drive up to Orlando to visit Disney's Animal Kingdom. I had originally intended to visit the park in 1999 during my senior spring break in college, but my vacation was derailed by a Big Mac extra-value meal at a Florida McDonald's that caused my gallbladder to explode. True story.

Animal Kingdom is the largest Disney theme park in the

world, sprawling over more than five hundred acres of lushly manicured grounds. One of the big draws is a roller coaster called Expedition Everest where riders evade the yeti on a high-speed runaway train. As we stroll into the Asia-themed section of the park, I'm blown away by how enormous and detailed the attraction is. I'm suddenly transported to the streets of Kathmandu, marveling at the backpacks and climbing gear hanging from the beautifully faked storefronts.

Like all popular Disney rides, the line is an attraction in its own right. Guests are gently corralled and then led on a labyrinthine journey with enough twists and turns that they never realize how long the queue is and consequently don't go completely insane. We snake through the purposely disheveled booking office and then out past an ornately detailed wooden temple. Finally, we wind into a building with an overhanging sign that reads "Yeti Museum." Inside, guests pass display cases containing news articles and relics from expeditions that have gone in search of the yeti. I call Brad on my cell phone. "Dude. I know where the yeti print belongs."

The process of actually getting the appropriate rep from Disney on the phone is harder than expected. No matter who I call or how I phrase my pitch, I sound like a crazy person. "Hi. So. I'm a professional monster hunter who found a footprint in the Himalayas that might be from a yeti. I was wond—Hello? Hello?"

I'm bounced from Burbank to Hong Kong, Orlando to Paris. Everyone hands me off to another department. Finally, on a last-ditch call to a publicist in Tokyo, I'm told, "You need to talk to Joe Rohde."

"Who's Joe Rohde?" I ask.

The silence on the other end of the line is deafening.

"Joe Rohde is the guy you need to talk to," the voice finally says matter-of-factly.

"Okay. Joe Rohde. Got it. Do you have a num—Hello? Hello?"

It doesn't take much digging to realize that yes, Joe Rohde is in fact, *the* guy. He is a senior vice president and an executive designer for Walt Disney Imagineering. As a first impression, know this: more than twenty years ago, when he and his small team were trying to sell Disney executives on the idea of an environmentally focused theme park (long before going green was chic), the question was raised as to whether live animals would be exciting enough for Disney's over-stimulated guests. To rebuff his doubters, Rohde paraded a 400-pound Bengal tiger into a board meeting. Needless to say, the terrified executives scrambled into a corner, and the question was dropped. He continued as the lead designer and developer for Animal Kingdom and was the driving creative force behind the Expedition Everest attraction.

If anyone is going to make this happen, it's him.

I contact Rohde's office and have the good fortune to not be hung up on by his lovely associate, Jennifer Gerstin, who either believes my story or is so bored at work that she's at least willing to listen to it. I tell her that we'd like to donate the print to the Yeti Museum at Animal Kingdom. She says she'll talk to Joe about it. I hang up, assuming that I've finally hit a dead end.

Jennifer calls back in fifteen minutes and says that Joe is interested. He hops on the phone, an unbridled bundle of energy coursing through the wire. "Where did you find the print?" he asks.

"In Nepal. In the Himalayas," I answer.

"Right. But where?" he wants to know.

"Oh. A few days' hike from Everest base camp."

"Where *exactly*?" he presses. He starts mentioning specific valleys and villages. I'm amazed. It turns out that Joe Rohde knows a lot of shit. We have a twenty-minute phone conversation that concludes with his offer to fly me to Florida so that I can deliver the print to him in person. And just like that, I'm going back to Disney World.

Meeting Joe Rohde in person is like meeting a lightning bolt. He's one of those magnetic iconoclasts who's probably a little bit crazy but in just the right way. When I'm introduced to him, he's wearing a bright Hawaiian shirt and a cowboy hat. Hanging from his left ear is a collection of strange earrings and charms of such substantial weight that his entire lobe is now stretched out to accommodate them. Walking around Animal Kingdom by his side is a trip. Despite the fact that he's genial to everyone we meet, Disney cast members are falling all over themselves in his presence. He's traveling with a bizarre entourage of individuals, among them a Kenyan safari guide who has been flown in for a meeting. Not only has the man never seen a theme park, but this is his first trip outside of Kenya. In the African-themed section of Animal Kingdom, I watch with delight as his eyes pop out of his head.

We arrive at Expedition Everest and pose for publicity photos where I hand the plaster footprint off to Joe. And then, with the formalities out of the way, we all ride the roller coaster. The Kenyan guy doesn't even know what a roller coaster is and spends the entire ride screaming with laughter. He loves it.

On the flight back to Los Angeles, I happen to be seated

next to Joe. We spend the five hours talking about everything from exotic foods to ancient weapons. I just do my best to keep up. "How much do you know about the use of armored dogs in Colonial Spanish combat?" he asks me. Up until this moment my only knowledge of armored animals is that polar bear from *The Golden Compass*. I decide not to mention this.

A month or so later, the footprint, a photo, and supporting materials are granted a thoughtful display located just before riders exit the Yeti Museum at Expedition Everest. I couldn't be happier about this. If nothing else, the print is a tangible connection to an important oral tradition. It is a twenty-first-century footnote to a saga nearly as old as the Himalayas themselves. I'm so glad that people can see it firsthand in the context of an attraction that brings the legend to life.

I spent a childhood enthralled by the magic of Disney. Peter Pan's ships carried me on my earliest flights, and my first expeditions unfolded on the exotic, albeit predictable, waters of the Jungle Cruise. This wanderlust of mine was surely conceived somewhere in the "world of yesterday, tomorrow, and fantasy." That Joe Rohde has seen fit to add my modest relic to Animal Kingdom has reminded me that Disney World is, quite literally, the place where dreams come true.

14: The Tourist Empire

Machu Picchu, Peru, 2009

It's as picture-perfect a moment as any traveler could hope for. A sun-dappled view of the cloud-framed plateau of Machu Picchu. Raising my camera, I hold my breath to steady my shot. Beams of light angle down through breaks in the sky; there's even a llama in the foreground munching quietly on lime-green grass. I'm going to win a Pulitzer for this. And then, without warning, an enormously fat woman in a Planet Hollywood shirt spills into the frame. The llama, as startled as I am, moves along. The photo is lost. A momentary image of the mighty Inca Empire dissipates, the ancient mountain city freshly conquered by an insatiable, seemingly unstoppable new superpower: tourists.

There is a very real distinction between being a tourist and being a traveler, and we should all aspire to the latter. Being a traveler means being an enthusiast, a vessel eager to be filled with the exotic. Being a tourist means checking off a prescribed itinerary, behaving like a sheep, and generally resisting the influences of the unknown in favor of familiar comforts. Citizens, this is a plea for sanity—nay, a call to arms! It's time for a revolution against the imperial forces of tacky travel. I submit to you that there is a better way.

When we travel, we don't just go someplace else, we also bring with us the place we're from. Whether we realize it, we are emblematic of our homeland. When we set foot in a foreign country, we inject our own presence into it, either adding flavor or poisoning the cultural water. And so I would like to humbly offer a little basic travel etiquette (and a tip or two on how to not be an international douchebag).

Let's start with wardrobe. I'm not sure when it happened, but at a certain point in history people collectively decided that in order to travel somewhere, they ought to wear a costume. The issue is perhaps most painfully illuminated on any trip to Africa. From Cape Town to Casablanca, the continent is under siege by colonialist khaki pants, beige epaulets, and floppy safari hats. If I see one more pasty-skinned Brit in a fedora ogling animals through a pair of oversized binoculars, I'm going to start frothing at the mouth. Look, I'm all for wickable fabrics, and, sure, I own my fair share of cargo pants; but if you're wearing a pith helmet or sporting a hunting vest covered in pockets, you better be able to take down a lion.

I'd also like to ask that, unless you're going to the beach, you consider leaving your shorts at home, guys. Beyond the fact that it is the easiest way to distinguish yourself as a tourist (men almost never wear shorts in their own country), I don't really want to look at your hairy legs. Not in a restaurant, never on a plane, and, for the love of God, never *ever* in a temple. Remember, you're an ambassador for your country. Throw some pants on, buddy. And, ladies, cool it with the tube tops in downtown Dubai.

While we're on the topic of sartorial choices, let's put a worldwide moratorium on shirts that read, "I survived (insert something totally survivable).ʺ Also, no more Joe's Crab Shack logos at the Wailing Wall or Ed Hardy patterns distracting from Picasso paintings in El Prado. Crocs are hereby banned from restaurants worldwide, and finally, I'm sure you loved your last trip to Paris, lady, but that bedazzled Eiffel Tower shirt is really f-ing up my view of the Acropolis.

However, if there's one touristic sin that makes me cringe above all others, it's this: the travel wallet. You don't carry a wallet around your neck at home, do you? No. You don't. So stop doing it abroad. It's the badge of an embarrassing paranoia and announces you as a complete maroon to every local you meet. You may as well be wearing a nametag that reads: "Hi. I'm not from here, and I think your country is full of criminals." You also advertise to the few actual thieves in town that your money is hanging openly around your throat. Perfect for a late-afternoon neck shanking. It's as simple as this: if you're too scared to keep your money in your pocket, you really shouldn't be out of the house.

Full disclosure: I'm terrible at foreign languages. Awful. After a combined eight years of Spanish classes in high school and college, I can barely order a burrito at Taco Bell. But even if you can't speak the local lingo, your efforts are always appreciated. Really. Use your overseas flight to learn some basics and struggle through as best you can. Expecting people to speak English in another country is ugly. As a side note, when you do have to fall back on it, speaking louder or with an accent will not make locals understand you better. "I need to go to the Marriott. THE MAAARRRRIIOOOTTT." The cabdriver is Greek, not retarded.

You cannot expect to eat the same way abroad that you do

at home. Nor should you. In fact, the human palate was meant
to stray beyond the confines of the local food court. Sadly, I've
watched Americans happily sit down for dinner at a Sbarro in
Moscow next door to an authentic Russian eatery. I've looked
on in horror at people choosing a KFC in Tokyo instead of any
of the six sushi restaurants on the block. The worst side effect to
gastronomical laziness overseas is that it encourages American
franchises to pop up in places where they fundamentally don't
belong. There's now a McDonald's across from the Pantheon
in Rome. And it's packed.

Food is knowledge. An hour in a local market tells the
story of a country. You can divine the climate, the economics,
and the character of a culture in simple baskets of produce, the
way a fortune-teller reads a palm. The scents of native spices
are languages that have hung in the air for generations, and a
butcher's choice of cut reveals time-honored values.

If simply looking at these foods is instructional, actually
eating regional cuisines can crystallize your entire impression
of a people. In Serbia, for example, the food is heavy and
prepared slowly, encouraging drawn-out meals that strengthen
familial bonds. The clay pots of slow-simmering Moroccan
tagines reflect the earthiness of the North Africans. Small plates
and family-style offerings of traditional Chinese dinners advise
a simple modesty.

Another way to completely derail your travels abroad
is to let someone else take the wheel. Oh, how I loathe the
many incarnations of "organized travel." An oxymoron of
the first degree. The idea of relegating one's discovery of
another country to the designs of a corporate booking office
or navigating foreign streets from behind the plexiglass veneer

of a tour bus should be a crime. In general, any vacation that hitches you to an ungainly group is just about the worst way of seeing a place. Nothing cuts down the intrigue of the rock-carved city of Petra faster than fifty Japanese in matching neon shirts led by a woman with a flag and a bullhorn.

When did we decide that travel should be so easy? Don't get me wrong, I appreciate a hotel with five stars on the doormat once in a while, and I can understand the temptations of comfort. After all, when we travel, everything shifts. Our whole world is knocked askew. The weather, the people, the language, the food, even the act of using the restroom. Foreign places can seem overwhelming, unwelcoming, and inaccessible. That's fair. But if you feel that way, take it as a hint that it's time to alter your approach. We have become far too expectant of our plans, demanding as little friction as possible from every moment of the journey. As travelers, it is our responsibility to adapt, otherwise we miss the whole point: the opportunity to gain a new perspective.

So break free. Dress smart, travel boldly, and try ordering your authentic dinner in the local language. America is in dire need of citizen liaisons, and with a little intrepidity, we can all be the travelers we were meant to be. The revolt begins now, friends. Do your part and fight back against the dreaded Tourist Empire.

CASE FILE: MINI MONSTERS AND JUNGLE DEMONS

NAMES: Chupacabra, Pombero, Tokoloshe, Icelandic elf, leprechaun, Kalanoro, Duende, Chullachaqui.

DESCRIPTION: Often humanoid, both in body type and personality, many with a streak of mischief, these diminutive beings are commonly heard but rarely seen. Some species wear little outfits (more on that in a moment). Several of these creatures, like the Kalanoro and Pombero, are classically described with "backwards feet," presumably an evolutionary survival technique to disorient potential trackers. The fiercest and most famous is the Chupacabra (meaning "goat sucker"), a vampiric beast with a spiny back and a serious grudge against livestock.

LOCATIONS: Worldwide. South America, Central America, Caribbean, North America, Europe, Africa, Madagascar.

STATUS: Some of these creatures, like the African Tokoloshe and Kalanoro, are very often described as troublemakers that enjoy playing pranks. Believers in the Pombero take this trait one step further, as he is rumored to actually impregnate women. Unplanned pregnancies and particularly unattractive babies are credited to the little beast (Bad Pombero. Bad!). In general, actual eyewitness sightings are sporadic, and very little compelling evidence exists in the form of video or photographic records. Although, in 2008, a dubious Argentinean home movie of a living garden gnome made quite a splash on the Internet.

The Chupacabra is touted as considerably more dangerous, blamed for thousands of animal attacks since he was first reported in Puerto Rico in 1995. He is now a fixture of nearly every nation in the Americas, and various individuals claim to have discovered his physical remains.

VERDICT: I've looked for a number of these creatures over the years, and most can be neatly tucked in a drawer labeled "Folklore." The Chupacabra is slightly more difficult to dismiss. With so many animals killed in unexplainable ways, there's at least room for more investigation here. In regards to the Chupacabra corpses that have been discovered, DNA testing nearly universally reveals them as garden variety canines with a severe case of the uglies. If the Chupacabra does exist, however, these mangy mutts are providing him with an excellent cover story.

Obviously, I'm open-minded about reports of strange cryptids roaming the earth, both big and small . . . but only up to a point. There are certain details regarding the mischievous monsters that are problematic for me. The Irish leprechaun is said to cobble his own shoes, and the Argentinean Pombero is said to don a red hat and carry a little knapsack. Okay. When tiny creatures have to go to some kind of mini-mall to buy clothes, I'm out.

15 : Чорнобиль

Ukrainey 2009

It started as a joke. A late-night, throwaway comment I made after one too many Red Bulls at the office. "What if we did a haunting episode at Chernobyl?"

It was considered by the rest of the group with the same gravitas as if I'd said, "What if we investigated an old synagogue with Mel Gibson?"

"What if we did?" someone countered. "Is it even possible?" After all, at this point we'd set a precedent by investigating the Suicide Woods in Japan, the Island of the Dolls in Mexico, and other unconventional locations. Our crew was also now well stocked with career travelers who love the sort of misadventure that *D.T.* dishes out. Our longtime MVP shooter (and Kenny G. hair impersonator) Gabe Copeland has filmed me from atop speeding buses, in rickety sidecars, and while swimming between unexploded bombs at the bottom of the ocean. Even he raises an eyebrow at the idea of going to Chernobyl.

It was a proposition not to be taken lightly. After all, the infamous meltdown at the Ukrainian power plant is the worst nuclear accident in the history of the world. Even the very word "Chernobyl" is toxic—laced with radiation, it seems.

The evening of April 26, 1986, was probably just like any other in the city of Pripyat. Many of the more than fifty thousand residents had finished their shifts at the power plant. It's unlikely that they observed anything out of the ordinary as they shuffled home in the chilly night air. City Hall was closed up for the evening, and guests streamed in and out of the nearby Hotel Polissya. A carnival had just been set up in a clearing behind the local gymnasium, and children were no doubt peering in at the bumper cars or gawking up at the bright yellow baskets swinging on the huge Ferris wheel.

Pripyat was a very young city, built only seventeen years before, but a railroad depot and cargo dock on the adjacent river ensured a vital link to Kiev. Early on, it boasted a unique and innovative architectural layout referred to as the "triangular principle." The design mandated that the tallest buildings be constructed along the circumference of the town so that, from any angle, an individual would have the perspective of free space. It was not this revolutionary design, however, that came to define Pripyat in the years to come. It was the power plant.

Chernobyl.

Heralded as a wonder of the modern atomic age and a symbol of Soviet engineering might. In an act of unbridled hubris, engineers even erected a statue of Prometheus stealing fire from the gods, which may now qualify as the single most ironic object on the face of the earth.

At 1:23 a.m., a systems check was initiated in reactor number four. Once this seemingly routine test began, a chain reaction of events was set into motion that would lead to global catastrophe. A fatal power surge caused explosions in the core of the reactor, and within minutes all hell broke loose.

To say that the fallout, which ejected into the atmosphere, was massive would be an understatement. Amazingly, the Soviets originally tried to mask the event altogether. That is, until a radiation alarm went off at the Forsmark Nuclear Power Plant in Sweden. *SWEDEN*. Go get a map. Look at Ukraine. Look at Sweden. Holy shit. The plume of radiation spread over half of Europe and parts of the Soviet Union, but Belarus turned out to be the big winner in this unlucky lottery by garnering as much as 60 percent of the lethal isotopes.

Since the sinister effects of radiation can take decades to manifest, the final death toll of the accident is hard to quantify. Clearly, though, the statistics are nothing short of tragic. Hundreds directly associated with the accident, the workers and first responders from the fire brigade, died from acute radiation poisoning within days. A UN report estimates that up to four thousand additional Europeans alive today might eventually perish from cancers caused by the accident. An even more disturbing report by prominent Belarus scientists working with Greenpeace predicts as many as a quarter of a million cancer cases and more than one hundred thousand fatalities.

In the immediate aftermath, officials refused to evacuate Pripyat at all, dragging their heels for a full twenty-four hours. But eventually they clumsily emptied the city, advising residents to leave their possessions behind, since it would be "safe" to come back in a matter of days. Nearly a quarter century has passed, and the city of Pripyat remains deserted, population: zero. The residents were never allowed to return. Five hundred years from now, this will still be an urban dead zone, unsafe for human occupation.

As for many abandoned places, there are long-standing rumors that Pripyat is haunted. Guards and the occasional visitor have recounted strange apparitions moving in the windows of the defunct hospital, sounds of children playing on the emptied streets, and phantom shadows climbing apartment building stairwells. Intriguing, to be sure. But was it possible to film there? Could one travel to the flashpoint of this atomic fiasco, walk into the heart of the city of Pripyat, and withstand the effects of the radiation for an entire night?

Our new team member, Jael, dove into research and placed a number of phone calls to Ukrainian contacts, and the officials at Chernobyl seemed more than willing to tell us that it could be done. But then again, the Ukrainian track record for atomic prudence isn't exactly unblemished. For their part, the executives at the Channel were appropriately freaked out by the idea, but we carefully explained that all of this was going to be completely safe. Which it would be, right?

The flight is brutally long, and I can't seem to sleep for more than seconds at a time. In the midnight hour we land in a daze and drive wearily into Kiev, a city that benefits from a veil of darkness. Our hotel is either built into the side of a whorehouse, or a whorehouse has been built into the side of our hotel. It's hard to say. I trundle past three of the most scantily clad women on the planet without even raising my head. I'm so exhausted I barely notice them.

Even though my room is about as cozy as a prison cell and I can hear pounding music from the bar downstairs, I still feel utterly at home. This is what it's like to work on *Destination Truth*. Adapt or be miserable. Wherever you are at the end of

a long day, you just pretend it's right where you want to be. I
hear a gunshot outside, close my eyes, and peacefully drift off
to sleep.

The gray light of morning finds us driving around the
concrete capital shooting B-roll and interviewing former
workers from Pripyat. These are hearty people. Stoic. They
mostly talk about the accident with a detached air, running
through the events as though everything has already been
said. Then their eyes float past me and out into the endless
apartment blocks of Kiev, a reserved sadness permeating their
gaze. Once enough questions have been asked and enough
remembrances forced to the surface, though, emotion begins
to bubble up, and color comes to their faces. They recall
their lives before the accident gradually, like a dream barely
remembered after a long, deep sleep. Due to time constraints,
few of these interviews will make it to air, which is a shame.
These are the real ghosts of Chernobyl. The citizens betrayed
by the very atomic power they tried hopelessly to harness
and then swept under the rug by the government who
commissioned them to do it.

We leave Kiev and drive sixty miles north. The landscape
is low and dull. For the most part, I hate it here. A large sign
by the side of the road—which I cannot read—advertises the
approach to what is known as the Zone of Alienation. Sounds
charming, doesn't it? The Zone is made up of three concentric
rings of increasing restriction (and radioactivity) around the site
of the disaster. The outermost zone is a full thirty kilometers
from the plant. Inside, a ten-kilometer ring contains the reactor
itself. The bull's-eye is Pripyat, guarded by a five-kilometer
enclosure. In other words, the accident forced the surrender of

an area sixty kilometers across. Within this ecliptic no-man's-land, human civilization has been forfeited; we've lost.

By midday we reach the first checkpoint, show our papers, and meet a military escort deputed to accompany us on our journey. The proceedings are tense, and at various points our translator and the guards with machine guns seem to be screaming at one another. Although in Russian, who can tell? It all sounds like Klingon to me. In the end, however, nobody shoots us, and we're allowed to continue. A metal gate creaks out a warning as it rises up, and we pass through the membrane of the outermost security ring.

Our escort, Yuri, is robust and camo-clad, with an awesome mullet and a sparkle in his eye. He speaks with a thick accent and seems like he's probably a funny guy, if only I could understand more than half the words coming out of his mouth. I spend much of the drive just nodding and smiling.

He assigns us three dosimeters, which are handheld devices that serve two functions. They calculate the sum total of the ionizing radiation with which we come into contact and, more importantly, sound a piercing alarm if we pass into an area of lethal exposure. Why he has only three of these, I have no idea. I strap one to my arm and look over as our cameraman Evan tapes one to the front of his crotch. "Yo, screw this, man," he says. "I'm not going to have my dick drop off." Fair point.

The first thing I'm struck by as we drive on into the Zone is how similar it looks to the rest of Ukraine. That probably isn't a good thing. The sky here has the same allergy to sunlight as the rest of the country, but other than the monochromatic landscape and complete absence of people, there aren't many indicators that we're careening into a nuclear wasteland.

To say that the outlying fringes of the Zone of Alienation are entirely empty, though, would be inaccurate. There are a few residents, mostly elderly, who have returned and reclaimed their former homes. They live within the outer Zone, far from Pripyat, amidst otherwise discarded villages. Underneath a light drizzle, we stop in one of these rural enclaves to interview a husband and wife. Their cottage, like so many others here, is slumped, its timbers exhausted after years of neglect. We walk up the steps into what feels like the opening frames of a horror film, and I'm shocked when the door bursts open to reveal two beaming, kind faces. They welcome us with kisses and firm handshakes, pulling us indoors and out of the rain. The interior of the house is also surprisingly cheerful. After leading us into the living room and seating us around a simple wooden table, they parade out various plates of food and a large, unmarked bottle of moonshine. To my abject dismay, I learn that the food has been grown in their garden. As I politely munch on carrots and beets, I imagine my thyroid gland and major organs silently failing. "This is delicious," I muster, wondering if my testicles will ever work again.

The liquor is harder to decline. The man insists that we have a shot with them. I want to explain that we can't. That we're on the clock here and that it's three in the afternoon. At the same time, you don't turn down booze in former Soviet states. It's just not done. So we have a drink. It tastes like ninety-three-octane gas and slides down my throat like a sanding belt. He refills the glasses. We drink again. He refills the glasses. I protest. He insists. I explain that we really need to start the interview. He insists. We drink again. He refills the glasses. This goes on and on.

Once we're all well lubricated, their story unfolds. The husband was a teacher who loved to teach. The wife was a nurse who loved to nurse. When the evacuation orders came, they took nothing with them. Their entire material life just vanished in an instant. It wasn't like moving to a new place, he explains, solemnly. It was a brutal interruption of their lives from which they never recovered. And so, after twenty years, and in the twilight of life, they wanted to heal that wound the only way they could. By coming home. He refills the glasses.

Once the interview is over, we merrily walk out into the street, slightly tipsy. Even the Zone of Alienation is looking good. The rain continues to come down, and before long we come to a collection of large buildings on either side of the road. A frozen statue of Lenin commands a barren park. "What is this place?" I ask.

"Administrative center. For workers," Yuri says.

I had almost forgotten that people still work here. A skeleton crew of employees maintain and protect the reactor, ensuring that it doesn't fall into further decay and, you know, destroy the world.

Yuri leads us across the street to the Chernobyl cafeteria for dinner. On a list of fine dining destinations, this has to be somewhere near the bottom. We're forced to step into a scanner surely stolen from the set of *Forbidden Planet*. It buzzes and beeps next to my head, which supposedly indicates that I'm free of deadly radiation, but for all I know this machine is more dangerous than the reactor. Inside the cafeteria, workers mill around the kitchen; almost nobody is speaking. I take my tray and walk down the buffet line, staring at irradiated pudding cups and atomic tater tots. I meekly

reach out and choose a plate of bright purple cabbage.
Bon appétit. We wash down our meals with a liquid dose of
something called ThyroShield, which is supposed to protect
our organs from radiation exposure. The label indicates that
it is to be taken "in a radiation emergency only." It is also
blueberry flavored, as though the flavor matters once you're in
a radiation emergency.

A few interviews follow. In the cafeteria we meet a guard
who claims to have seen strange lights just the night before.
We also meet several former residents who describe ghostly
figures of friends and family members who died either in the
accident or from poisoning in the years that followed. Several
eyewitnesses report bright orbs of energy and the sensation of
being followed through the decaying public buildings. They
seem rattled about their experiences, and we jot down the
locations of their sightings for further investigation.

Across the street we enter a nondescript lodge that's kept
open for visiting officials, scientists, and idiots like us. You know
that feeling when you check into a motel room, and you're
instantly certain that a porno turned murder suicide happened
there? You look down at that crusty duvet cover, convinced
that it's thoroughly caked in blood and semen. This is like a
radioactive version of that—times a million. My unassailable
adaptability is at a breaking point. There isn't a single surface
in the room that I want to touch, and once I take my shoes off,
I'm almost immobilized by the idea of having to walk across the
carpet. I feel like Howard Hughes in a porta-potty. I stare at the
showerhead for nearly two minutes before deciding that bathing
here is completely out of the question. If I had a roll of Saran
Wrap, I'd go *Dexter* on this place. Since I don't, I lie down on

top of the bed and try not to breathe. If there's one consolation to this night, it's that tomorrow will be much, much worse.

In the morning, we drive on under the perennially gray sky. At the ten-kilometer checkpoint we undergo more scrutiny and suspicious stares before eventually being permitted to pass. More lonely roads. Weeds writhing up through cracked veins in the asphalt. Nature is slowly disassembling this world. Along the way we pull over and walk through a former soccer field, which now serves as a permanent parking lot for trucks and tanks that were used to fight the fire at Chernobyl. Passing the bleachers, Yuri uses a Geiger counter to sweep the air in front of us. Simply approaching the vehicles, the needle begins to quiver and whine. As he waves the sensor near the tank treads, the readings go off the charts. The dosimeter on my arm suddenly screams out, and we retreat. Back on the road, the rest of the crew seems depressed at the treadmill of gloom that keeps rolling by, but Yuri is simply beaming.

"Isn't this amazing?" he blurts out.

"What is?" I ask.

"This! You're an American. Twenty-five years ago you would not be here. You understand. We shoot you!" he laughs out.

I laugh too. Not sure how else to react.

"But now, here we are. Ukraine and America. Together!" he says, shaking his own hand.

He's right, of course. It *is* amazing. I had nearly overlooked the symbolic significance of our presence here. Though Moscow's iron rule has dissolved, the culture of isolation and institutionalized silence is taking time to rewrite itself. The tense checkpoints and sideways glances are merely the icy remnants of our still-thawing Cold War. The workers who spent their lives keeping this place a secret must look upon my group with deeply mixed emotions. Yuri smiles and pats me on the shoulder. It's just a little moment. A gesture not captured on camera. But warm enough to soften an entire wasteland outside the window.

The scenery soon turns apocalyptic. We pass by gutted buildings and a lethal river choked with listing, half-sunken ships. The rows of barren trees thin out, and in the distance looms the iconic reactor number four. The fortified ventilation stack that rises up from the nondescript-looking building is immediately familiar to me from news footage, file photos, and the occasional nightmare. The sight of it sends a shiver down my spine, and I glance over at the dosimeter on my arm, watching the digital readout for signs of elevated radiation. The plant grows larger through the windshield, as does my level of disbelief. We park no more than 1,500 feet from the reactor. I step down from the car and hear the dosimeter on my arm react quietly. "Don't be alarmed," Yuri says with a grin. "Radiation levels slightly higher here but safe for short periods." Crazy bastard.

My crew and I are informed that we're not allowed to film the reactor from certain angles, which means one of two things: either these folks are insane enough to believe that someone might want to steal their top-notch nuclear technology, or the reactor is falling apart and they don't want anyone to notice. Guards quickly usher us into the annex building.

Most of us, at one time or another, have had terrible, terrible jobs. For me it was a stint as a waiter at a doomed Japanese supper club in Beverly Hills where I peddled cut-rate sushi to a seemingly endless parade of aging Hollywood harpies. Toiling away at these sorts of ignominious gigs, we tend to ask ourselves the question: *Who has the crappiest job in the world?* Well, my friends, I've now met him. Rat exterminator? Sewage worker? Tollbooth operator in North Dakota? No. Those would be child's play compared to this. Inside the operations building I'm introduced to a guy who holds the title of "Official Chernobyl Reactor Photographer."

Let me explain this. Once a month this poor son-of-a-bitch has to don some sort of *Andromeda Strain* suit and walk *into* the Chernobyl reactor. Once inside, he videotapes the structure to document the failing integrity of the building. It's so radioactive in this joint that when he's done, he has to eject the tape and just leave the video camera on a table (adding it to a pile). After he exits the building, his clothes are destroyed, and he's scrubbed down with harsh chemicals. While he's describing all of this to me, I can't help but notice a whole host of kooky tics and weird mannerisms that appear to be completely out of his control. At any rate, he goes on to explain the state of the reactor, and I do my best to listen while thinking about whether I'm going to have to shake his hand at the end of this (I am, and I do).

In the wake of the accident, a hastily conceived concrete sarcophagus was erected around the nuclear reactor. It restrains the more than two hundred tons of uranium and plutonium remaining inside the building (only about 3 percent of the deadly radiation escaped in the accident). This superstructure began to fail within five years of its installation, and today it is cracked, leaking, and expelling radiation into the atmosphere. It has been estimated that an earthquake of six or more on the

Richter scale could collapse the sarcophagus altogether, leading to an outright global emergency. With the USSR dismantled and Ukraine flat broke, it falls to the neighboring nations to address the issue. An ambitious new engineering plan calls for the construction of the largest movable structure on the planet: a twenty-thousand-ton steel shell that would slide over the current sarcophagus. But for now that's all it is. Just a plan. If it's left undone, we may, in time, be doomed to an encore performance here. A prominent Russian scientist was quoted as saying that "the next Chernobyl will be Chernobyl itself."

We leave the well-irradiated staff behind for the final leg of our journey, the road to Pripyat. The final checkpoint involves inspection of our vehicles and passports, although the whole thing feels surprisingly cursory. I can't understand what the guards are saying, but I imagine that it's along the lines of "What the hell. You made it this far. You're obviously crazy. Come on in."

The road into the center of Pripyat is long and straight. On either side, apartment buildings stand like silent sentinels. Most of the windows are blown out, and inside of the individual rooms, my attention is kidnapped by the sight of furniture, paintings, and tattered drapes. It's like a hundred dioramas of destruction. We stop at the end of the road and step out into the city center. My mouth falls slightly open. In front of me, City Hall. To my right, a department store, the Hotel Polissya, and a long street beyond. To my left, rows of buildings. It looks endless. "Josh," someone in the group calls, "the radiation suits."

Right. We open the back of the van and unbox eight full radiation suits. They're baggy and heavy and smell like talcum powder. The plexiglass hood is hot and uncomfortable. I feel

a bit like Marty McFly in this thing, but who cares? This is
no time for vanity. Every little bit of protection helps. The
dosimeter is now ringing steadily and has to be recalibrated to
a higher setting. We're now absorbing radiation all the time; it's
up to the meter to let us know when we've had enough. Once
we're suited up, we get to work. Nothing, and I mean nothing,
can touch the ground here. Anything set down gets left behind.
Every camera is wrapped in plastic and fortified against the
unusual elements.

We start by exploring the old hospital. We know that many
first responders died here and that several guards have claimed
to see phantom patients in the building. We enter the hospital
through broken windows on the ground floor. Once inside, I'm
gob-smacked. The halls and rooms are filled with furniture,
gurneys, papers, and medical artifacts, giving the place a
terrifying character. We make our way room by room and floor
by floor, being careful not to touch anything and to avoid the
dripping water seeping from the floors above. The dosimeters
ping occasionally, reminding us that our time here is finite.

Our investigative equipment is uncooperative inside the
hospital. My thermal imager stutters and powers itself on and
off. Batteries seem to discharge in minutes, and the night-vision
cameras become finicky. Since radioactivity shouldn't affect the
gear, we're left unsettled by the malfunctions. Along with just
being creepy, it's also a frustrating experience for us, since we
have to rehab the electronics through thick gloves and partially
fogged faceplates. Once we get everything up and running
again, we slowly ascend a staircase to the next level. We wander
through various exam rooms, passing under antiquated surgical
lights and around old obstetrics tables. A thick patient register

lists hundreds of procedures that were carried out here. Across the hall I shine my light into a pediatric ward and rows and rows of rusting cribs. For a moment I think I catch sight of a person in the window. Just for an instant. It's probably a reflection, I tell myself.

Room after room of blackness fills my periphery, partially obscured by the edges of the mask. At the top of the next stairwell, I turn the corner to see a human shape in the thermal display. I just about jump out of my skin and yell to Evan to point the camera down the hall. Nothing. I'm baffled. The image on the thermal appeared to be a person leaning out from a room or from the wall itself. We search up and down the hall, but despite our best efforts, we can't replicate the reading or find any explanation as to what the device picked up on. We hustle into the back part of the building to keep searching, but the area turns out to be hot with radiation. We're forced to make a hasty retreat from the complex at the urging of our dosimeters.

It's well past midnight as we make our way behind City Hall, and I try to shake off the figures I thought I saw in the hospital. There isn't much time to reflect, though; one horror quickly begets another here. The night-vision camera reveals what our eyes cannot yet see: the massive skeleton of a Ferris wheel. We move into an open yard and the decomposing remains of the dark carnival. Our flashlights flicker across the steel cadavers, and I can't help but feel like the crew from the *Nostromo* exploring the remains of that lonely alien spaceship. Support struts from a partially collapsed Tilt-A-Whirl fan out like bony ribs, and the great wheel looms over us like a giant. Jael goes to examine the bumper cars, but I remain

near the wheel, transfixed by, of all things, the ticket booth.
I'm suddenly thirteen and basking under the honey yellow
lights of the carnival that passed through our small town each
summer. Just past the whirling Gravitron ride, I'd stand on my
tiptoes to see over the ticket booth counter, a dog-eared copy
of *Something Wicked This Way Comes* sticking out of my back
pocket.

Back at Chernobyl, I can hear only my breath inside the
heavy radiation mask, and Bradbury is ringing in my ears:
"Death doesn't exist. It never did, it never will. But we've drawn
so many pictures of it, so many years, trying to pin it down,
comprehend it, we've got to thinking of it as an entity, strangely
alive and greedy."

Jael yells out. She thinks she sees someone sitting in one
of the bumper cars. I run over to her at about the same time
our medic, Rex, images a heat signature in the second floor of
a nearby building. The dosimeter screeches. The bumper cars
are too radioactive, and we race to follow the thermal hit. The
ticket booth recedes behind us.

Our last stop is the elementary school. It's visually
overwhelming. Homework on desks dated April 26, 1986. A
basketball stranded on the gymnasium floor. In the library
we walk on a carpet of books that have long fallen from their
shelves. Pages tear under our boots. In the music room, we
fiddle with an old piano, tapping out a dissonant chord. As we
move into the next room, all of us hear a soft tinkle of keys as
the piano sounds out behind us. Every hair on my neck stands
on end. We run back, but the piano is lifeless.

The strange activity increases as we get deeper into the
building. In one of the classrooms, I think I see a thick shadow

behind Jael that causes me to reach out, accidentally hitting her in the face. The tension of this place and the discomfort of the suits are unbearable. We're all on edge. Moments later, Jael screams and runs out of the building after feeling as though something has grabbed her hand. Shortly after, the dosimeter alarm goes off, indicating that, like a roast in the oven, my team and I are done. It's time to get out of here before we get overcooked.

At the van, we carefully peel back the radiation suits, which will later be burned. We pile in and drive through all of the checkpoints, into the dawn. Halfway to Kiev, we pull over at a cheap motel and rent three rooms for an hour. We all take hot showers and scrub our skin until it's ready to bleed. Most of our clothes are thrown into the trash can. We emerge reborn. For the first time in days, the sun even peeks out through the clouds.

Can the unprecedented level of radioactivity provide a scientific explanation for what people are seeing in Pripyat? Or is there something else? Is Chernobyl haunted? I believe it is, in a sense. After all, ghosts are a semblance of life. A trace of existence. There are few places on earth where modern civilization has been reduced to memory. What remains here is a specter of the past and a warning for the future.

Chernobyl haunts us with the reminder that all of man's ambitions are ephemeral. Our grandest designs and sturdiest monuments, fleeting. Waves of exhausting sadness came over me at Chernobyl. It's the side effects of exposure, not to radiation but to deafening silence. It forces us to face an uncomfortable truth: that we are all simply ghosts in waiting.

16: On the Subject of Ghosts

Jiankou, China, 2009

Shining my flashlight in front of me, then behind, all I can see in either direction is the endless stone ribbon of the Great Wall. I'm freezing my ass off up here. It's the middle of winter in Jiankou, China, and the wind is whipping up over the crumbling ramparts, making my crew and me fairly miserable. My feet slip and slide on icy cobblestones that have been wholly neglected for the last five hundred years.

The Great Wall of China is a construction effort without equal, a monumental barrier designed to close off the entire northern frontier of China from Manchurian and Mongol invaders. It is the single largest man-made object in the world, stretching for more than 3,100 miles. The top of the wall is wide enough that ten men could march along it shoulder to shoulder. Regularly spaced multilevel guard towers interrupt the span and were once fully garrisoned with soldiers.

Though the project required generations to plan and execute, from where I'm standing, the placement of this particular section seems utterly ill-conceived. Where the original builders encountered natural obstacles in the form of jagged mountains, rather than, "Oh, I don't know, go around," they simply built over them, undeterred by topography (or the laws of physics, it seems). The result is an improbable stone line that zigzags up and down like a General Motors stock graph. This part of the wall is so unnaturally steep that it's referred to as "Eagle Flies Facing Upward." With the way I keep slipping, though, it'll soon be renamed "Josh Falls Facing Downward." The area is incredibly dangerous and has been closed to the public entirely.

As haunting stories go, this one is pretty straightforward. It has been estimated that as many as a million people died building the Great Wall of China; many of their bodies were reportedly interred in the stonework itself. Locals have attested to visions of phantom soldiers as well as a malevolent energy that possesses people to jump to their deaths. Add the fact that several visitors have died mysteriously, and you've got a compelling story on your hands.

Eventually, we make our way into the highest guard tower that locals believe is paranormally active. The shelter of the tower interior cuts the wind and feels comparatively warm. We wander through a few empty stone rooms, peering out through arrow slits at encroaching fog. Walking around the central chamber, I feel Evan's hand on my back. This isn't uncommon, since at night we wear large backpacks with cameras strapped to them, and every hour they need to be tended to. I assume that Evan is changing out a tape as he jostles me around. I quietly ask what he's doing and shudder when I hear an answer from twenty feet away. I spin around and, sure enough, he's nowhere near me. *Nobody* is near me. I suddenly feel sick. I've just been touched by nothingness.

My good friends Jason Hawes and Grant Wilson from

Ghost Hunters tell new investigators that they will be "hit, punched, grabbed, slapped, and pushed" by things they can't see. The idea being that if you hunt for ghosts long enough, one of them will eventually reach out and smack you. But even though I've experienced the same phenomenon that they so often describe, I remain an entrenched paranormal skeptic. That's probably a good thing. Like Jason and Grant, I don't think every creak and moan is a ghost. If I did, I'd have the same investigative acumen as Shaggy from *Scooby-Doo.*

Why am I a skeptic? Well, let's talk about the problem first and then the promise. There are a number of pretty staggering assumptions we have to make as paranormal explorers. The first assumption, of course, is that there *are* ghosts. Or at least there might be. We're ostensibly looking for some sort of entity or presence that is able, on some level, to manifest itself in the physical world.

The next assumption we make is that ghosts mainly come out at night. People ask me all the time why we only conduct paranormal investigations after the sun goes down. The answer is simple. Statistically, more ghost sightings are reported after dark. This is a good thing, too, since it makes for better television. Nobody wants to watch me hunt for ghosts at Pompeii at three in the afternoon while an Italian guy sells gelato in the background. But as to whether there actually is more paranormal activity at night is certainly up for debate.

We make further assumptions through the use of a variety of equipment. We use thermal imagers in the field because there's a school of thought that states if ghosts are able to manifest themselves, they must emit some sort of energy or heat. But again, this theory is backed by precious little evidence. We use audio recorders to conduct EVP sessions. "EVP" stands for electronic voice phenomena. These are background recordings that, when amplified, are supposed to reveal paranormal speech. Thomas Edison first proposed the use of sensitive audio recording equipment to capture these sounds from the beyond in a *Scientific American* article. In the one hundred years since, the technique has been widely used. The results can be compelling but are largely open to interpretation.

Finally, we assume that ghosts like to hang out in places where death or great tragedy has transpired. We don't hunt for ghosts at a Chuck E. Cheese's. If this measure is a just one—if the dead congregate in places where life has been extinguished—then I've certainly been in a position to see ghosts. Over the course of my tenure on *Destination Truth* I've visited some of the world's most tragic addresses. I've spent the night alone atop the desert fortress of Israel's Masada, where nearly one thousand Jewish zealots committed suicide. I've wandered through the oldest coliseum of the Roman world at Pompeii. Within this stone girdle, untold numbers of people were put to death in unspeakable ways. I've walked the lonely shores of Easter Island, tempting powerful Polynesian spirits, and rapped one-on-one with King Tut himself in the deserts of Egypt. Hell, I've even looked for ghosts at the bottom of the ocean amidst the twisted wreckage and skeletal remains of a Japanese fleet from World War II. The point is, I've spent a lot of long nights investigating the Grim Reaper's Greatest Hits. And still, I can't say for certain if ghosts exist.

All of our assumptions speak to the larger problem: the methodology of paranormal research is largely experimental.

This is probably going to be an unpopular statement to some die-hard fans, but looking for ghosts isn't exactly scientific.

Take the great magician Harry Houdini, who was obsessed with the paranormal. As someone who plied his trade convincing audiences of his supernatural abilities, in the latter part of his career he devoted his time to debunking so-called spiritualists. He made a deal with his wife, Bess, that after his death, he would try, for ten years, to communicate from the other side. At yearly séances, Bess would work with mediums attempting to glean a code known only to Houdini and his wife. On October 31, 1936, the final séance was held on the roof of the Knickerbocker Hotel in Hollywood. The code remained unspoken and Bess Houdini reportedly said, "My last hope is gone. I now reverently turn out the light. It is finished. Good night, Harry!"

While we can't really call Houdini's method scientific, he gets points for trying to prove that the afterlife is real. But when it comes to ghosts, proof is hard to come by.

Hypothetical example: If, during the course of an investigation, the Ghost of Christmas Future walked out from a solid brick wall and waved a scythe and a bony finger at the camera while bolts of lightning shot out from under his hood, it would not constitute proof of anything. Nada. Zip. Not unless one could coax him to appear again and again. The real world of paranormal encounters has no such regularity. No Headless Horseman—the decapitated Hessian soldier who can be relied upon to appear nightly on a covered bridge. Without this, there can be no hard science.

Science involves gathering empirical and measurable evidence, forming hypotheses, and testing said hypotheses.

There must be *repeatable* results in order to draw conclusions. Oh, and the testing has to be wholly objective and conducted in a controlled environment. Without a demonstrable connection to the other side that can be studied and written about in peer-reviewed journals, the pursuit of paranormal truth will always be marginalized by science.

So if our methods for seeking the truth behind paranormal claims are so experimental, why bother looking at all? Well, according to a recent CBS News poll, 48 percent of Americans believe in ghosts. That's more people than those who support Darwin's theory of evolution. And what's more, one in five people believe that they have personally seen or been in the presence of a ghost. If we conclude that a legitimate ghost sighting would constitute proof of an afterlife, 20 percent of Americans would therefore have witnessed a miracle.

And isn't that sort of a big deal? In the previously mentioned poll, a broader question revealed that a staggering 77 percent of people believe in some sort of life after death. And despite the fact that there's a clear overlap between religion and the paranormal, television networks are loath to make God a part of the conversation. Heaven forbid that spirits and spirituality be uttered in the same breath.

So why avoid the connection? Quite simply, because it's so immensely polarizing. A whopping 87 percent of people who believe in the afterlife believe that science will never prove if it exists. This statistical chasm is exactly why inquiries into the paranormal are vital. Faith and doubt have bubbled in the human mind since primitive tribes first worshipped animistic tokens and fertility idols. The search for ghosts is inescapably tied to the search for meaning, explanation, and divinity.

Irrefutable proof of the existence of spirits would rattle the foundations of our society. So, yes, it's worth looking for them.

On *Destination Truth*, we may never prove the existence of ghosts. Without one of those smoking toasters from *Ghostbusters*, we certainly won't be able to capture one. But what we are doing is listening to those who have had compelling experiences and then trying to substantiate their claims or explain them as best we can. It's not exactly science. But it does *nag* at science. Fierce debate and unconventional thinking have always underscored the history of scientific discovery. We're simply contributing to the ongoing conversation.

Half of us believe. Half of us do not. Where do you stand?

17: Tourists and Pharaohs

Egypt, 2009

Egypt is a den of thieves. Let's get that out in the open right off the bat. Having gone toe to toe with some of the planet's most hardcore hagglers, touts, and cons, I put Egypt in a class all by itself. Which is to say, I love this place. Anyone who has traveled with me can attest to my genuine affection for all manner of well-attempted tourist molestation. During my last visit to Cairo, I was in the country for two minutes and thirty-seven seconds before someone attempted to rip me off. And the guy who tried was working for passport control. Kudos, Egypt. Good to see you're keeping up that sterling reputation.

I had just stepped off a flight from Dubai and was standing in line to buy a tourist visa. It wasn't a promising sign that visas were being administered by a dude at an airport bank, rather than a government office. An enormous and weathered sign to my left read, "Visa: $15 U.S." The lone teller looked up at me and said, "Hello my friend. Price is two hundred Egyptian pounds." As a point of interest, anyone in a financial transaction who calls you "my friend" who isn't actually your friend is usually about to twist a proverbial knife into your back. A little quick math in my head revealed that this price was more than double what was listed on the sign. "I thought it was only fifteen U.S. dollars," I said.

Behind the teller, a loitering Egyptian police officer flashed a crooked smile at me and winked. So much for the cops.

"Okay. Fine. Fifteen dollars," the teller relented.

After I gave him a twenty-dollar bill, he then argued that he had no change in either currency. At a bank. He had no change at a bank. You've got to respect anyone with the balls to even attempt that kind of move.

Beyond passport control is one of Egypt's classic scams. I call it the "hotel shuffle." Here's how it works. A con wearing an official-looking "Visitor Assistance" badge walks up to an arriving tourist and asks if he needs a hotel for the night. Few people show up in Cairo without booking accommodations ahead of time, and so the tourist invariably explains that, no, he already has a room arranged. The con then tells the traveler that he's happy to call the hotel and have them send a complimentary shuttle. Most tourists are unnerved at the sight of the salivating mob of cabdrivers outside and take the man up on his seemingly generous offer.

Then, like a lamb to the slaughter, the unassuming tourist is led into a tiny office where the con artist calls the hotel. Except that he doesn't call the hotel. He calls an accomplice. After speaking in Arabic for a few moments, the man informs the tourist that the hotel has no record of his reservation and is fully booked. The alarmed mark then jumps on the phone; the fake hotel agent apologizes for the mix-up but confirms that there is no record on file. Alternate lies include that the hotel is undergoing renovation, has flooded, or is suddenly out of business. Luckily the con happens to know another hotel with vacancies (where he gets a healthy kickback for diverting our bewildered tourist). Pretty awesome, huh?

I shook off no less than three people who offered to call my hotel for me and then emerged into the throbbing heat, humidity, and screams of a hundred taxi drivers. "I take you to Marriott for eighty pounds," someone yelled.

"You're hilarious," I offered back. "Twenty pounds."

The cabbie smiled. "Okay, my friend. We go."

"Great. And I don't want to stop off at your friend's store," I added.

"Quick stop. I know wonderful price on rug."

And this is how it goes in Cairo. By the time you get to your hotel, you're tired, sweaty, possibly stabbed, and occasionally in possession of an overpriced oriental carpet. Here are a few actual exchanges from my last visit to the city.

Hotel Concierge: "I can arrange a private car for $500. Is okay?"

Me: "No, is not okay. As I understand it, your job is to help me, not screw me."

Hotel Concierge: "How does fifty bucks sound?"

Guy at Memphis ruins: "My friend. Good camel. You want to buy?"

Me: "To own?"

Guy: "Yes, my friend."

Me: "How old is it? It looks old."

Guy: "Thirty-seven years, sir. Very strong."

Me: "Thirty-seven years? Don't these things die at, like, forty years?

Guy: "Yes. But will fetch good price for meat at butcher."

Guy at Pyramids: "How much for your bracelet?"
Me: "Not for sale."
Guy: "I give you two of my best postcards for it."
Me: "Wow. What about if I throw in my watch for five postcards?"
Guy: "Yes, my friend! We have a deal?"
Me: "We do not."

Guard: "I take your picture for one dollar."
Me: "Okay, but I get to hold your gun."
Guard: "Be careful. It's loaded."

All of this endless scamming exists, of course, because Egypt is a powerfully magnetic tourist destination and is featured on just about every traveler's "bucket list." The endless influx of mostly upper-class vacationers accounts for more than 15 percent of the country's entire GDP. Add the fact that the average Egyptian nets less than $5,000 a year, and it's easy to see how more than a few of the twenty million people in Cairo turned into Fagin from *Oliver Twist*. To make matters worse, the entire country is an infrastructural disaster. After they erected the greatest civilization in the history of the planet, it's as though the Egyptians said, "Okay. That's enough. Let's just call it a day for the next five thousand years."

The modern capital city that sprang up in the tenth century A.D. has outgrown itself many times over and is now a bustling mess of dust, grime, and human energy. Trying to drive through Cairo is like being trapped inside an Arabic version of the video game Paperboy. Camels, babies, women in burkas, runaway construction equipment—you name it, and it's drifting out into the middle of the street. Enough to distract even the most focused of commuters.

In short, Egypt takes the silver medal in the Exhausting Destination Olympics (India still dominates the podium). But for those hearty enough to sidestep its pitfalls, it's also one of the crown jewels of adventure travel. The people, even the ones ripping you off, are as warm and hospitable as any I've met, and they have a deep-rooted passion and pride for their collective past. There are places where travelers get a vague sense of history and places where history reaches right out and punches you in the gut. Egypt's treasures are not just relics consigned to dusty shelves or remnant architecture on otherwise modernized city streets. The entire country is an open-air museum of the first degree, as vast and substantial as the desert dunes themselves. From the temples at Abu Simbel to the mighty Sphinx, visitors are ultimately humbled by a scale of antiquity seldom seen.

As we prepare to bring *Destination Truth* to Egypt, I'm cautious, to put it mildly. It will be more than a year before the three-decade dictatorship of Hosni Mubarak comes crashing down and the country rises in rebellion. With my previous excursions to Egypt as prologue and political tensions simmering, my critical hackles are up when it comes to toting our cameras to the Land of the Sun. Our first order of business is therefore to hire a top-notch "fixer." For those unfamiliar with the term, fixers are native producers hired to facilitate the logistics of overseas productions. Able to speak the indigenous language, navigate local politics, and draw upon their own Rolodex of contacts, fixers can be indispensible assets to filming in foreign countries. In Egypt, they're a downright necessity.

If the experience of getting through customs here is difficult as a tourist, just imagine what it looks like when you show up with twenty cases of expensive film equipment. Case in point: a few months before our arrival, another popular travel show headed to Cairo to film and never made it out of the airport. Literally. Unable to negotiate with airport officials, the entire production was turned around and forced to leave the country.

Intent on actually clearing the terminal, I search high and low for an Egyptian producer who can dial into our needs and help us navigate the road ahead. A trusted producer friend insists I call a man named Ramy Romany. When I ask him why, I'm told, "Just call him. He's the guy."

Ramy is the son of Romany Helmy, one of Egypt's most respected fixers. As motion picture and television production crews flooded into Egypt like locusts in the last half of the twentieth century, Ramy's father positioned himself as a big player in this business. Ramy and his sister are the next generation; together with their family, they have produced more than five hundred projects for the BBC, National Geographic, Discovery Channel, and countless other companies.

When I first call Ramy to suss out his abilities vis-à-vis a rather unique expedition, he answers the phone in what could pass for a velvety British accent.

"How can I help, Josh?"

"We're hoping to accomplish a number of activities in Egypt, and some of them might be . . . difficult," I say.

"Such as?" he hums calmly.

"I want access to film the Tut Mask at the Cairo Museum."

"Not a problem."

"I also want to be able to film at the Pyramids."

"Not a problem."

"I also want to—"

"Josh," he cuts in. "What do you *really* want to do?"

I pause. "What I really want is access to King Tut's tomb in the Valley of the Kings. Alone. At night."

Silence on the line. "That *is* a challenge," he admits. "Give me an hour."

The discovery of the tomb of Tutankhamun is one of the most thrilling stories of modern archaeology, and the ensuing legend of Tut's curse may be one of the most romantic. In the early 1900s, Egyptologist Howard Carter, sponsored by his patron Lord Carnarvon, toiled in vain for six long seasons in the Valley of the Kings. After more than five years of nearly fruitless excavation and the shifting of tons of sand, Carter's funding and support hung by a thread. And then, on the fourth of November, 1922, under the shadow of the tomb of Ramses VI, a step was discovered. By the next day twelve more stairs and a sealed entrance were revealed. On the verge of history, Carter sent a frantic cable to his sponsor: "At last have made wonderful discovery in valley; a magnificent tomb with seals intact; congratulations." Nearly three weeks later, on the twenty-fourth of November, Carnarvon arrived with his daughter, and the dig resumed.

Once all sixteen stairs were cleared, the fully exposed door revealed several intact seals, one of which bore the name Tutankhamun. In the following days the door was opened, leading to a twenty-six-foot passageway and interior door. In his journals, Carter wrote, "At first I could see nothing, the hot air escaping from the chamber caused the candle flame to flicker, but presently, as my eyes grew accustomed to the light, details of the room within emerged slowly from the mist, strange animals, statues, and gold—everywhere the glint of gold. I was struck dumb with amazement, and when Lord Carnarvon, unable to stand the suspense any longer, inquired anxiously, 'Can you see anything?' it was all I could do to get out the words, 'Yes, wonderful things.'"

The tomb itself is surprisingly small, and Tut is believed to have been a relatively minor ruler. The real significance of Carter's find is that, unlike every other royal tomb in the Valley of the Kings, which had been plundered bare, Tut's was largely undisturbed. For the first time, the world bore witness to the full splendor and wealth of a pharaonic burial. The antechamber alone yielded nearly seven hundred objects, including disassembled chariots and ornate beds. The inner chamber housed four gilded shrines, a multilayered sarcophagus, and the famous golden mask.

Whisperings of the Pharaoh's Curse began almost immediately. At the moment of the tomb's discovery, all the lights in Cairo were said to flicker. Shortly after, a cobra, the symbol of royal rule, was discovered lurking in Carter's house. Several months later, Lord Carnarvon died "mysteriously" after a shaving nick on a mosquito bite became infected. It was declared thereafter that any person who disturbed the tomb of Tut would fall victim to the powerful and ancient curse. While as many as a dozen other people connected with the discovery of the tomb did suffer early deaths, many workers present at the tomb's discovery suffered no ill effects, and Carter himself lived to the reasonable age of sixty-four before dying of natural causes.

Though the factual fabric of the curse may be showing

a few holes, the myth of Tut's wrath continues to echo down through history. Our own interest in the story stemmed from curious recent events that transpired when a team of specialists moved Tut's body for a CT scan. One researcher's vehicle nearly ran over a small child on the way to the site, the state-of-the-art equipment malfunctioned in the presence of the mummy, and a storm kicked up over the usually peaceful valley. Many Egyptians still hold to the belief that these are signs of the infamous curse, and we took this as the perfect opportunity to test the merits of a purportedly three-thousand-year-old vengeance. That is, if I could get inside the tomb.

Good to his word, in one hour flat, Ramy calls back with promising news. He thinks he can arrange a private date with the most famous pharaoh of the ancient world. We land in Cairo and are met by Ramy Romany. His mane of black hair goes well with his dark suit and flashy smile. Ramy is a coil of enthusiasm in a rail-thin frame. He knows absolutely everybody in sight, shaking more hands than a politician in a primary. In the streets, Ramy parts a sea of rabid taxi drivers and airport hustlers like a modern-day Moses and throws me the keys to the beautifully beat-up Land Rover of my dreams. I could get used to this guy. We discover a *Drifters—Greatest Hits* cassette in the glove compartment and groove into Cairo. Because nothing says ancient Egypt like the dulcet tones of "Under the Boardwalk."

We drive straight to the Egyptian Museum. For those who have never set foot in this place, it's a complete sensory overload and, in a literal sense, the worst museum on the planet (which makes it my favorite). A depository disaster without equal, this is like God's garage—if God were a hoarder. There's no way to overstate the obscenity of volume within the

107 halls of this sprawling warehouse. There is zero regard for presentation; packing crates, dusty treasures, and precariously placed statues occupy every square inch of available space, teetering boxes piled to the ceiling. I shit you not, you could literally get killed by a falling mummy in here. Half of the displays aren't even labeled. The immensely significant Palette of Narmer, a five-thousand- year-old siltstone relic, sits by the front door and is given all the presentational gravitas of a bag of Doritos in a 7-Eleven. Most people walk right by it, unaware that they just ignored one of the oldest hieroglyphic inscriptions ever discovered.

Ramy has arranged for us to film Tut's death mask and is able to get us into the museum a full thirty minutes before it opens to the general public. This is a blessing, since the museum routinely suffers from a crushing sea of tourists that literally spills through the gates like a great wave the moment the doors open. After ushering us through a side entrance, Ramy motions us to wait patiently, as we're not the only ones to come into the museum early. It turns out that Dr. Zahi Hawass is giving an interview on the second floor.

Hawass holds the position of secretary general of the Egyptian Supreme Council of Antiquities. If that sounds like an impressive title, it is. Hawass administers all of Egypt's excavations and is personally responsible for allowing, denying, and overseeing projects all over the country. Though he is a polarizing figure who undeniably enjoys the media spotlight, Hawass has probably done more for Egyptology than the pharaohs. He's established order over the thousands of archaeological sites, passionately advocated for a new museum, and worked to institute a culture of historical preservation across the country. He also directed the recent CT scan on Tut and has attested publicly to his unwillingness to dismiss the power of the curse.

Once Hawass vacates the museum, my team and I are turned loose. The experience of being alone here is such a privilege. The normally bustling galleries are eerily silent, and the sound of our footsteps echoes through the main hall. There are no shoving crowds, no shouting guides, and no snapping cameras. Under the watchful eye of megalithic statues, I roam past endless cases of papyrus fragments, gold coins, and mummified remains.

On the second floor, the spoils from Tut's tomb take up most of the atrium. We navigate past Tut's reassembled chariots and shimmering golden shrines into room three. Here, in a glass case, is the singular symbol of Egyptian antiquity: the death mask of Tutankhamun. I can hear the guards downstairs opening the front doors, and I know that in a matter of minutes this gallery will be bursting at the seams. But in the fleeting silence I stand face-to-face with a golden portrait of the boy king. His obsidian-and-lapis-lined eyes convey a distant yet unmistakably powerful gaze that is utterly hypnotic. After my moment of zoning out in the gallery, Evan interjects. "Um, Josh? Can you move?"

"Sorry," I say, jumping out of the way. "Shoot it!" The team films fast and furiously as the sound of hundreds of footsteps rumble up the stairs.

After our visit to the museum, we make our way across town to the Giza Plateau to take in the iconic Pyramids. Here's the thing about iconic places. After repeated exposure to these legendary locales and objects in magazines, in movies, and on postcards, it's always amazing when they still manage to inspire awe in person. I'm similarly amazed when these touristic golden calves turn out to be deflating letdowns. Incidentally, my three-way tie for the most disappointing up-close icons on earth are:

- **The *Mona Lisa*.** Even if you do manage to get past any one of the six million people a year that crowd into the Louvre to see Da Vinci's masterwork, be prepared to be kept at bay by airport security dividers and a thick veneer of bulletproof glass. And the kicker: the painting is only twenty inches long.

- **Mount Rushmore.** First of all, it's in the middle of nowhere—the Black Hills of South Dakota. The real problem, though, is that once you're close to it, the monument looks downright silly. The megalithic busts sit above a sloping pile of loose rocks. They look like they're perched atop a hill rather than commanding a mountain (get whatever *North by Northwest* fantasy you have out of your head). More importantly, the proportions are wrong, and the execution is all-around sloppy. Also, it's hard for me to get too worked up over a public-works project on seized Indian land that was carved by a card-carrying member of the Ku Klux Klan. I'm just saying.

- **The Hollywood Sign.** We all know the nine white letters that overlook the Hollywood Hills from more movies than we can count. The problem? In real life, we don't see them via a swooping helicopter flyby. Instead, we view them from afar, and unfortunately, they look tiny. When friends come to visit me, they always ask where the Hollywood sign is. I point up into the hills and watch them squint, inevitably, in disappointment.

On the other end of the spectrum, there are a number of contenders for best in-person jaw-dropper. The Taj Mahal really is a staggering monument to love, Angkor Wat in Cambodia is all it's cracked up to be, the Grand Canyon is incomprehensibly bonkers to behold, and the Christ the Redeemer Statue above Rio will knock your socks off. But for me, the choice is simple. The Pyramids at Giza.

Yes, the Giza Plateau sits on the western edge of Cairo and isn't as remote as you've been led to believe. Yes, the site is crawling with guys selling camel rides, papyrus hawkers, and scammers galore, but it doesn't matter. With each step toward these four-thousand-year-old marvels, it's impossible to resist the urge to shake your head in disbelief. More than two million limestone blocks make up these otherworldly monuments, the only surviving member of the Seven Wonders of the Ancient World. The scale, symmetry, and flawless execution are simply beyond comprehension.

We tour the Pyramids and speak with a few officials before setting off to our true destination: Luxor. The city appears out of nowhere, hugging the wide and gentle east bank of the Nile like a desert mirage. Compared to the frenetic chaos of Cairo's endless alleys, the relative serenity of Luxor's broad streets is dramatic. Originally known as Thebes, this once shimmering capital city is now a stunning playground of ruination. Across the river, the desert landscape rises up into a breathtaking escarpment, concealing the Valley of the Kings.

The Luxor Temple shares common borders with the city's main street and a colorful market. Replete with larger-than-life statues of Ramses II and the remains of massive courts and halls, the temple manages to retain immense dignity even under the weight of so many gawking tourists. It's easy to overlook the adjacent Avenue of Sphinxes just outside the temple. This cobblestone corridor, originally lined with more than 1,300 human-headed sphinxes, once connected the Temple of Luxor to Karnak, more than three kilometers away. Today, only about seventy of the graceful statues have been excavated. The rest are literally buried beneath the modern streets of the city.

We have an uncharacteristic patch of downtime in Luxor, and I hop a cab to the temple complex of Karnak. This sprawling enclave spans a staggering two square kilometers, and the largest structure, the Temple of Amun, is one of the largest religious buildings ever constructed. Once inside, I make straight for the Great Hypostyle Hall.

If there's a runner-up in Egypt to the Great Pyramids, this might well be it. Dominated by 134 thick papyrus-shaped columns that rise up like gigantic stone reeds, it was designed to emulate a massive swamp. In antiquity, the hall would even flood with several feet of water when the Nile overflowed, a spectacle that I imagine with great pleasure as I weave between the pillars.

Back in Luxor, we depart for the Valley of the Kings from the eastern shore of the Nile. Past throngs of dockside merchants, we cast off in a felucca, a traditional wooden sailing boat, which will ferry us to the opposite shore. From the middle of the Nile, it's possible, if only for a moment, to find respite from the tourist hordes and aggressive hawkers. Here, between the banks, there is a brief and ephemeral silence that reveals the natural splendor of this place.

Since we've been granted permission to enter the Valley of the Kings after it closes to visitors, we're under our own steam. No air-conditioned buses or organized tours for us. Once across the river, we transfer our many cases of gear to camels to continue our journey.

As anyone who has seen *Destination Truth* can attest, I really hate camels. And before you start writing me letters about how they're masters of the desert and one of the planet's evolutionary wonders, save your breath. I've heard it all before. They spit, they bite, they're uncomfortable to ride, and they're utterly uncooperative. Many people aren't aware that there was once a North American camel, which went extinct. Take that as a lesson, modern camel: we can survive without you, and you should really check your attitude.

With our gear and crew atop our stupid camels, we make our way through the relentless afternoon heat and into the Valley of the Kings. With a stream of tourists headed out of the Valley, we once again find ourselves in the unique position of having a little piece of Egypt all to ourselves. As much as this seems like a rare opportunity, I've come to learn that it doesn't have to be. And as with many realizations, they involve my dad.

As mentioned earlier, I'm from a small town on the north shore of Massachusetts, Manchester-by-the-Sea. That's the actual name of the town. Three hyphens. The place is like a series of Norman Rockwell scenes that have been stitched together and brought to life. Every morning, my father wakes up at about four thirty, starts his truck, and drives to the little village at the center of town. He buys a cup of coffee and sits on a bench by the pier, where he shoots the breeze with other "townies." These are lobstermen, retirees, and other professional insomniacs who like to start their day before the sun. On the rare occasions when I'm jet-lagged enough to join my father on his morning ablutions, I'm struck by something. The Manchester-by-the-Sea of 4:45 a.m. bears no resemblance to the Manchester-by-the-Sea of 10:45 a.m. The cast of characters, the sights and smells, are utterly distinct. There is a stillness to those in-between hours, a meditative peace to the dawn that evaporates with sunlight, a solitude to dusk that is consumed by night. It's a private place where we seem to have infinitely more clarity of purpose.

Years ago, on my first trip to Egypt, I eschewed the Great Pyramids in favor of an early-morning drive to the Pyramids of Dahshur. Only a few hours south of Cairo, these pyramids are some of the most spectacular in the world and are plagued by only a fraction of the mob at Giza. I jumped out of my car just before sunrise and was, by a long mile, the very first pilgrim to the site. I walked past a closed ticket booth and up the dunes, hearing only the sound of sand slipping beneath my feet. I approached the pyramids as the last man on earth and found myself moved not only by the view but by the magnitude of my isolation. I walked around and around the massive structures, laying my hands on the base stones and listening to the morning breeze. Eventually, a guard on a camel galloped up and told me that the site was not yet open. Good-natured, though, he dismounted, leaned his machine gun against the base of a pyramid, and proudly described the history of the structures. We got lost in conversation for a while and eventually turned in unison toward the valley below, disrupted by the sound of three enormous tour buses kicking up dust on the horizon. The morning quiet had only just arrived and yet expired in a moment.

Now, as the sun sets beyond the Valley of the Kings, I'm reminded of Dahshur and of Manchester-by-the-Sea. I'm here outside of the sun's supervision, in a half-lit world. The silence of the valley is profound. This is, after all, a massive necropolis, a burial ground for Egypt's most powerful pharaohs. Florence Nightingale once called it "the deathbed of the world." The wind slips through the canyons; the many tomb openings appear as black punctures in a beige canvas in the failing light. We set up our gear just outside the exterior gate of KV 62, the Tomb of Tutankhamun.

Once the sun has set, we begin to power up our equipment. As we prepare to enter the tomb, a guard appears, and we introduce ourselves. He smiles, takes my hand, and places an ordinary key into my palm. I'm dumbstruck. Just like that, I'm holding the key to King Tut's tomb.

I head back to our base camp, where, just as we're about to begin the investigation, a high-pitched wind picks up. I glance back, startled by the loud flapping of tarps tied over a nearby excavation site. Above us, a horizontal blanket of sand whips over the escarpment and hails down onto our group. We scramble to cover our monitors and shove cameras under our shirts in the blinding sandstorm. And then, in an instant, it's over. Stillness retakes the canyon, and we're left staring at each other, shaking dust out of our clothes. The superstitious would call this the breath of Tut himself, warning our group to keep a distance. As I look down into the sooty tomb, I'm not sure I disagree.

In the outer courtyard I squint at photo displays of Carter

and his team on the threshold of discovery. We pass down the staircase and narrow corridor that ends at a thick metal door. I slip the key into a weathered padlock and jump as the tumblers click with a snap. The door opens with a high creak, and as I step forward, I meet Tut himself. Though not nearly as shimmering as his gilded mask, the man is no less impressive. Small in stature but big in presence, he lies under a layer of glass, his hair, teeth, and facial features still well preserved after thousands of years. A sobriety has set in amongst our group, and we move in reverence through the antechamber.

The room beyond is brightly painted with scenes of Tut wandering through the afterlife. Black-eyed gods stare in silent judgment. On the far wall are vivid paintings of twelve monkeys representing the fleeting hours of the night, a message to my team and me that we had better get to work. We string cameras throughout the chamber and proceed to conduct isolation sessions in front of Tut's mummy. If there's any truth to the legend that anyone who dares disturb the tomb will feel the wrath of the pharaoh, crowding him in his own grave is as good a trial as any.

My isolation session is actually a little overwhelming. I have my teammates lock me into the tomb and then retreat to the surface. The heat and humidity make my clothes feel sticky, and I sit on the ground, staring ahead into nothingness. Behind me, the lifeless body of Tutankhamun is giving me goose bumps. Alone, without any light, in my mind I try to reconstruct the walls and hieroglyphics. In this tiny subterranean chamber, the darkness and silence conspire to reveal Tut's tomb through the eyes of Carter, Carnarvon, and the ancient Egyptians themselves.

Finally, my eyes seem to focus on something, a sliver of

light just outside the chamber. At first I think it's someone from my crew, but a walkie-talkie check reveals that they're all huddled at base camp. The image is soft and unformed but luminescent. I can't quite discern a shape, but I'm rattled. Rising and staggering toward the slats of the exterior metal door, I reach out my fingers as the light extinguishes.

To this day, I'm not sure what I saw down there. Maybe just a trick of the eyes. But maybe not. While the logical side of my brain doubts my senses, the legend of Tut's curse is so bewitching that I don't have the heart to dismiss it. It seems silly to me sometimes that a boy who's been dead for millennia should hold any sway over us, but if I'm being honest, when I was alone in that blackened tomb, there was a part of me that felt sorely afraid of the still-mighty Tutankhamun.

Egypt is, in the end, a place of striking contrasts. It is a country in a state of youthful revolution, yet rife with old-guard corruption. It is also forever hewn to its ancient past, caught between the chaos of car horns and the silence of the sands. Its graceful monuments are overrun with khaki-clad armchair adventurers and wall-to-wall elderly travelers on some sort of a golden-years farewell tour.

A common tip from career adventure travelers is usually to move against the masses and sidestep the world's more obvious destinations and swim against the tourist current. But with the right attitude, a keen eye on your wallet, and a little early-to-rise ingenuity, you can have it both ways in Egypt. Tourists and pharaohs. You just have to submit to the stream, for better and for worse. Lest you miss one of the greatest shows on earth.

Postscript

It was clear from the longing gazes exchanged between our tech manager Sharra and fixer Ramy that there was a yet to be written chapter from our Egyptian expedition. And not long after we returned home—a matter of months, actually—Sharra announced that she had fallen in love. An engagement and wedding followed, and on August 18, 2010, Sharra and Ramy welcomed into the world Sophia Marie Romany: the very first *Destination Truth* baby and—who knows?—perhaps the next generation of international monster hunter.

CASE FILE: *MOVIE MONSTERS*

NAMES: *Dracula, the Mummy, the Wolfman, and the Creature from the Black Lagoon.*

DESCRIPTION: *These cryptids come right off the silver screen and are the collective property of Universal Pictures. Although the red carpet is their primary domain, versions of these celebrity monsters have actually been reported in the real world for years.*

In 1931, Bela Lugosi donned the infamous black cape and fangs to play the lead in the film version of Dracula. *Perhaps his performance would not have been so historic, however, had it not been for the deep belief underlying Bram Stoker's tale. There are references to vampires dating back more than a thousand years. Said to possess a corpse or be transferred from one soul to another courtesy of a seductive bite, vampires are reported to be nocturnal creatures with long hair, sharp fingernails and teeth, and an insatiable appetite for blood.*

In 1922, producer Carl Laemmle heard news of Howard Carter's discovery of King Tut's tomb and the legend of the Pharaoh's Curse. Ten years later, The Mummy *was shot partly in the Mojave Desert, with the eponymous villain portrayed by Boris Karloff.*

In 1935, Henry Hull starred in Werewolf of London. *Six years later, Lon Chaney Jr. starred in* The Wolfman. *But the legend of lupine beasts with a lunar aversion was actually born centuries earlier in the powerful folklore of pre-European cultures.*

Werewolves are described as hunched shape-shifters with a pronounced muzzle and, of course, a serious unibrow. In Argentina, it is believed that the seventh son born in a family is destined to become a lobizón, or werewolf.

One of the first 3-D movies to be released in the States, Creature from the Black Lagoon premiered in 1954. Real-life sightings of similar reptilian monsters paint him as a seven-foot-tall upright creature with scaly skin and glowing red eyes.

LOCATIONS: Eastern Europe, Egypt, the Amazon, Argentina, the United States.

STATUS:

Vampire: The legend is an old one, but as recently as 2004, superstitious villagers in Romania came to believe that a deceased local man was a vampire. They dug the unfortunate body of Petre Toma out of his grave, cut open his chest, removed his heart, burned it, and then ingested the ashes. So much for resting in peace.

Mummy: Reports of the Pharaoh's Curse have been carried on the wind since Carter first cracked open Tut's tomb. Even the head of Egypt's Supreme Council of Antiquities, Zahi Hawass, has spoken about exercising caution during excavations so as not to elicit curses. Workers on current excavations in Egypt are still notoriously superstitious, some refusing to disturb the entrance to newly discovered tombs altogether.

Werewolf: In remote corners of Eastern Europe,

the legend of the werewolf continues to inspire terror. In Argentina, fear of the <u>lobizón</u> prompted a law stating that every seventh son be baptized by the president of Argentina, who then becomes an honorary godfather to the child. This tradition continues to this day.

The Creature from the Black Lagoon: In 1988, a young man named Christopher Davis reported a sighting of a Lizard Man near Scape Ore Swamp in Bishopville, South Carolina. He claimed the creature mauled his vehicle and that he barely escaped the monster's wrath. The incident created a media frenzy in the small town and gave rise to a local mascot. In 2008, resident Dixie Rawson's car was viciously attacked, causing some to believe that the swamp creature had returned.

VERDICT:

Vampires: Currently experiencing a resurgence in pop culture, this age-old myth is underscored by paranoia and an inherent fear of evil, demonism, and impurity. But really, the only thing you should be scared of is accidently wandering into one of those <u>Twilight</u> films.

The Mummy: In Egypt, the <u>Destination Truth</u> team put the Pharaoh's Curse to the test and was assailed by a mysterious sandstorm. I'm not saying the curse is real, but one of our producers did fall ill in the Valley of the Kings. Plus, I still have grains of windblown sand lodged in my underwear.

Werewolf: Stories of these hirsute creatures stem from Old World beliefs and predominant superstitions about wolves that began as early as the seventh century B.C. Though the etiology is disputed widely, it has been attributed to everything from an explanation for serial killings to the misdiagnosis of mental disabilities.

Creature from the Black Lagoon: We ended up calling the story of South Carolina's Lizard Man a hoax. Other tales of humanoid reptiles strain credulity for even the most open-minded monster enthusiast. Reptilian men may be scary, but evidence suggests they're nothing more than the terrors of Tinseltown.

18: Amazonia

Brazil, 2008

The world around me is utterly alive. As our jeep lurches over the badly mangled roads of Brazil's interior forests, I have the sensation that I'm traveling inside a massive living organism — which, of course, I am.

It's the kind of environment where, no matter how prepared you are, it doesn't take much for the tables to turn. This is one of the last great wildernesses on earth: nearly two billion acres of intertwined jungles and rivers named after the fierce and exotic female warriors of Greek mythology, and just as dangerous. In this species-rich ecosystem, we don't have to travel far to run into some of nature's most lethal predators. In fact, we're actually looking for two of them.

The first is the giant anaconda. Even the garden-variety version can grow in excess of fifteen feet, but this long-rumored recluse said to inhabit the tributaries of the Amazon is reported to be more than double that. We fly west to Manaus, a derelict boomtown perched at the intersection of the Amazon and Rio Negro. In the nineteenth century, this was the gilded empire of European rubber barons who made a fortune extracting the jungle's natural latex. Despite the isolation of the city, wealthy business owners erected lavish estates and even constructed an opera house to the tune of $10 million. It is said, however, that half the singers of a visiting opera company died of yellow fever before their first performance. Eventually Manaus fell into disrepair but is today undergoing an eco-traveler renaissance. Even the opera house is back in operation, after sitting underneath a dim marquee for nearly a hundred years. (Singers are also now properly vaccinated.)

We begin at the Instituto Nacional de Pesquisas da Amazônia. Here we meet with Dr. William Ernest, the coordinator of biodiversity research. The doctor illuminates the difficulty of proving (or dismissing) the case for the giant anaconda, reminding us that the Amazon basin is about the size of the entire continental United States. Less than 4 percent of this behemoth ecosystem has been scientifically cataloged or systematically explored.

At the nearby Manaus Snake Research Center, we meet with Dr. John Francisco, a herpetologist and veterinarian. He tells me that, while many consider the existence of a giant anaconda unlikely, it is biologically possible. He also offers to give an up-close look at one of three anacondas in captivity at the facility.

The process of observing the anacondas is questionable from the start. I'm asked to descend a ladder into a partially flooded pit with Dr. Francisco and two other specialists. Once we get to the bottom, I hang back and let them do the work of coaxing a ten-foot predatory snake out of the water.

Any illusion I had about safety goes right out the window as the men break into an impromptu Three Stooges routine. They're slipping, bumping into one another, and generally not catching a snake. Eventually they manage to subdue one of the angry serpents and invite me over to help hold it. The snake is thick and powerful, and has a broad head with an intimidating jaw. I ask the doctor how many times he's been bit; he beams and replies, "Never."

Not five minutes later he's pointing out the extremely sharp and numerous teeth on the snake (stop me if you know where this is going) and, *of course*, the snake snaps at him. In an instant the doc's index finger is inside the snake's mouth, and the other two guys rush to pry it open and release the bloody digit. If a herpetologist at a snake research center can't control one of these things, what chance do I have?

Nearly all eyewitness sightings of the giant anaconda take place deep in the jungle interior, which means we're going to need a boat. We proceed to the docks and charter the paddle ship from the *Steamboat Willie* cartoon. Setting a course and steering the enormous vessel away from the city, we begin to glide along the glassy waters of this four-thousand-mile-long river.

We go ashore in a small village and interview an eyewitness named Damien who tells us about a nearly one-hundred-foot snake that thrashed his boat and forced him into the water, where he swam for dear life. In another encampment we meet Elias, who tells us that he watched a fifty-foot anaconda coil around his friend, dragging him below the surface. The men sound terrifyingly sincere, and as we hike to a clearing near the site of the most recent attack, I'm suddenly filled with trepidation about being out here after dark. We set up base camp at 8:00 p.m. and manage to run into a snake by 8:37 p.m. It's not an anaconda. In fact, it's probably worse. It's tiny, maybe a foot long, and sitting at eye level on a branch near our camp. One of our local guides spots it. "Dangerous," he whispers. "No antivenom."

Later in the evening, Brad spots a pair of eyes on one of the IR cams. We sweep the area and, just under my flashlight beam, I see something turn over on the ground. It's an anaconda. Not giant, but certainly big enough to make me jump back. We wrangle the snake and measure it at just less than ten feet. I'm also careful to not put my fingers too close to its mouth. Shortly after, the rain forest lives up to its name and sheets of water explode out of the sky.

I spend much of the next day swaying in a hammock on the lower deck of our boat as we steam farther and farther from civilization. We come to an aboriginal village and meet the chief and his family. He explains that he heard the sound of barking one night and ventured down to the shore to see a more-than-sixty-foot snake slithering up the bank. The head alone was three feet long, he insists.

That night we search the area, hiking on land and motoring the tributaries in a wooden banana boat. Flashes of lightning help us to scan the surface of the otherwise murky water. Suddenly we see something slip into the river near the bank. We steer the boat over, and four of us jump into the water, clutching around in the shallows. In moments we manage to haul a fifteen-foot boa constrictor up onshore. It's absolutely huge and so powerful that our combined effort can hardly subdue it. Still, it's not a giant.

Shortly after, the sky pours down again, destroying two cameras while we scramble to get the rest of our gear back to the boat. I drop beneath the deck to get into something dry. By the time I return topside, the rain has relented. In the still night air, huge javelins of lighting drop down from above. Looking out over the railing of the boat at the flickering jungles, I'm reminded that some monsters are all too real. I'm relieved to be away from the snake-infested rain forest but mindful that tomorrow will bring an all-new adventure.

As I scan the blur that's passing by the car windows, I can make out rows of scarred trees bled by rubber workers collecting their precious sap. The laborers who carry on this nearly 3,500-year-old tradition do so in small, isolated groups. Alone within these illimitable rain forests, these laborers have been telling tales of a creature called the Mapinguary for centuries.

I speak with various individuals throughout the afternoon as we trek from one remote location to another. The workers seem agitated when talking openly about the creature and nervously describe a hairy, black, bear-like animal that is both highly elusive and yet dangerously aggressive toward humans. Some claim it has only a single eye, others say it has a mouth on its stomach. Everyone agrees that it smells terrible.

By late afternoon we've pushed our way deep into the forests for a meeting with an indigenous tribe whose stories mirror those of the rubber tree workers. With hundreds of different clans and more than two hundred unique languages still whispered here, I've chosen my local translator carefully. These tribes are among some of the wildest left on earth. More than fifty of them have almost no interaction with the modern world. Just two years ago, a low-flying plane traveling near the border between Brazil and Peru was actually shot at with arrows by what may be one of the last completely uncontacted groups in the world. A few hazy photos taken from the aircraft show agitated villagers covered head to toe in rich red and black pigments, firing wooden bows skyward. And two years ago, members of the Kulina tribe reportedly killed and ate a local farmer in a ritualistic act of cannibalism.

We park the 4x4 and cross a simple footbridge into a village clearing where I'm half certain I'm going to be cooked in a stew. Baskets of animal skulls are hanging from the porches of various huts, and a group of hunters sharpen their arrows on the fringes of the encampment.

The inhabitants turn out to be more than amiable, though, eagerly greeting me with a wooden bowl of fire ants, which I'm obliged to consume. I do my best to hide the burning pain in my mouth and just keep smiling and chewing.

After the snack, I sit down with the villagers and hear their tales of the dreaded Mapinguary. Their descriptions of the creature sound suspiciously like that of a giant ground sloth, which did live alongside humans here about ten thousand years ago before going extinct. One of the competing theories about the Mapinguary is that the ground sloth has somehow survived in some isolated pocket of these jungles.

More interesting, however, is the belief that the Mapinguary is an ancestral memory—a recounting of actual run-ins between humans and giant sloths, passed down in an unbroken chain for thousands of years.

One of the most striking aspects of the stories is a common claim that the animal is able to mimic the human voice. When pressed to explain this, the workers say that if you yell out, the Mapinguary will return your call. In other words, the creature is an echo. A reverberation from the massive tangled skein of

vegetation that is the Brazilian Amazon. Cut down too many
trees or mistreat the sacred land, and you will incur the wrath
of the Mapinguary, they say. To these people who live by
the balance with nature, the animal is revealed as a sentinel.
Like the yeti of the Himalayas, the fairies of Ireland, the
Taotaomo'na of Guam, and other such cautionary creatures, he
is an age-old guardian. A spokes-creature for environmentalism
dreamed up millennia before the word even existed.

Suddenly I'm struck by the rain forest itself. From the
center of this clearing where we're sitting, it now appears to
me as a mighty wall rising up around the circular periphery of
the village like a battlement. My translator is communicating
back and forth, trying to sort out the details of one elder's
experience, while I imagine what it must be like to live here
after dark. Once the sun goes down, that ring of forest will spark
to life, a cacophony of sounds emanating in stereo from the
labyrinth beyond. And as I look at the many children huddled
curiously behind our cameras, wide-eyed with fear at the
mere mention of the Mapinguary, I can see that he is also part
boogeyman. Just like the giant anaconda, he is a foreboding
representative of the unforgiving power of the wilderness
beyond the village, ready to envelop anyone who missteps. As
the sun sets and shadows grow long, I begin to feel the power
of these creatures for myself. The night is coming on fast, and
I'm not sure if I'm chasing legends, memories, or dangerous
animals. The many versions of the legends are beginning to
coalesce and work on my nerves like a campfire ghost tale. And
perhaps that's the point of telling them—to put people on edge,
which is about the safest place to be in the Amazon.

CASE FILE: *SUPER-SERPENTS*

NAMES: Giant anaconda, Sucuriju Gigante, Mongolian Death Worm, Rainbow Serpent, Hoop Snake, Nabau, Tatzelwurm, Lambton Worm, Yuxa, Nirivilo, Naga, Quetzalcoatl, Seps, Apep, Joint Snake.

DESCRIPTION: These are, to put it succinctly, bad-ass snakes. Snakes that some of the most prominent cultures in history have revered and feared. Many are described as stretching out in excess of one hundred feet, with surely proportionate sets of fangs. However, a few of these intestinal-looking monsters are actually known less for their length and more for both their aggression and their formidable defense mechanisms. For example, at only five feet long, the Mongolian Death Worm is said to kill by spewing acid or electrocuting its foes. And people say size matters.

Quetzalcoatl, a feathered serpent from Mesoamerican culture, is a card-carrying Aztec god. His domain includes reproduction, rain, lightning, thunder, and agriculture. Quite a to-do list. In Australia, the Rainbow Serpent is believed to control the flow of the earth's water. Apep, an evil basilisk in Egyptian folklore, rules over darkness and chaos. And, of course, that infamous serpent in the Garden deceived poor Eve.

LOCATIONS: The Amazon, Mongolia, Japan, Egypt, American West, Colombia, Venezuela, Ecuador, Peru, Bolivia, Brazil, Trinidad, Paraguay, Argentina.

STATUS: There's something primal about our fear of snakes. Maybe it's hardwired into our cultural DNA. Whatever the reason, I don't see anything wrong with a little bit of ophidiophobia. Even Indiana Jones was afraid of them, and he was brave enough to appear in <u>The Kingdom of the Crystal Skull</u>.

It should therefore come as no surprise that stories of large, terrifying, super-snakes easily gain traction. Case in point: just a few years ago, an Indonesian zoo reported capturing the largest snake in history. Shaky amateur video seemed to back up the shocking claim that this colossal reticulated python was nearly fifty feet long, and the story spread like wildfire on cable news.

Also, in February of 2009, two photos surfaced of an enormous snake cruising through the Baleh River in Borneo. A member of a team monitoring flood conditions from a helicopter supposedly snapped the images. When released, it sent Indonesian communities into a tizzy, as they immediately considered it a Nabau, the mythical serpent famous in local Iban legend.

VERDICT: At the Indonesian zoo, the super-snake was reassessed, at which point the so-called largest ever documented came in at just a bit over twenty feet long. Impressive but nowhere near a world record.

The aerial images of the swimming snake in Borneo have also come under fire. It's not a good sign that the photos were submitted anonymously and, even more troubling, that there were only two of them. If you saw a waterslide-sized snake from the safety of a helicopter, wouldn't you take a few more shots? Who snaps two photos and goes, "Yeah, that's probably enough. I'm pretty sure I got it." The glaring problem with the images, though, is the color of the water, which doesn't match the river in Borneo. Using a reverse search engine, a Kansas librarian matched the picture to a waterway in the Congo, not the Baleh River, and discovered that the photo had been doctored. Case debunked.

If there's one place in the world where a super-snake could exist, it's the Amazon. Dozens of tribes believe they have seen the giant anaconda, and their stories are remarkably consistent. The lack of definitive proof of the creature can be somewhat forgiven, since the waters of the Amazon are the most impenetrable on the planet.

To date, the largest snake in the world is a reticulated python. A hefty specimen can measure more than twenty-five feet in length. (The largest one ever recorded was just under thirty-three feet long.) The New York Zoological Society has a standing offer of $50,000 for a live snake thirty feet in length or greater. So far, there have been no takers. Then again, how the hell would you get that thing through LaGuardia?

19: Travel Will Save You

In Cambridge, Massachusetts, there's a travel agency with a sign on the door that reads "Please go away. Often." More than just a catchy motto, this seems to me a rare piece of honest-to-God truth in advertising. A snarky suggestion that perhaps it would be best if you just left. It's a slogan I wholeheartedly support. Any of us can overstay our welcome in our own country, like a too-drunk groomsman at a wedding.

A scant 25 percent of U.S. citizens have a passport. That means that most Americans haven't seen the world's great monuments firsthand or known the blissful anonymity of strolling exotic city streets. Most people have no idea what hummus is *supposed* to taste like or felt the ego-busting helplessness of not being able to read a single sign in a Chinese bus station. They haven't left the country.

There are, of course, many reasons for this. Not everyone can afford to travel, and those who can don't always have the time. In general, employees in the United States are granted less vacation time than citizens of almost any other Western country. Many Americans simply opt to travel domestically out of necessity. To say nothing of the fact that America truly is a diverse travel destination in its own right. But there is, I suspect, something more dangerous at work here.

The 75 percent of Americans who don't travel abroad have any number of other excuses why. Some are scared to travel. One of the great American prejudices to reblossom in the last decade is the belief that many people in the world would love to kill us. It's rubbish, of course. There are all of about four places where you're likely to get your head blown off, and it's not as though you're going to accidentally wander into any of them. Nobody unwittingly plans a honeymoon to Tora Bora or finds their flight to Cincinnati suddenly rerouted through Sierra Leone. If there's one common chord that any career traveler can strike, it's this: people are pretty lovely. From Tacoma to Timbuktu. In fact, the more exotic, impoverished, and generally unseemly the location, the more hospitable the residents tend to be. And our commonalities are many. Beyond customs and norms and wildly variant beliefs, we all generally laugh, cry, and make our way along the dusty road of life in pretty much the same way.

To those who eschew travel because of how "horrible" it is to fly, I reserve my greatest ire. Bunch of babies. When did we get so collectively myopic about the miracle of aviation? Has flying become a little less plush over the last couple decades? Sure. So what? You're still getting slingshot over the globe at half the speed of sound. People pine for a "golden age" of aviation when planes had spacious legroom, drapes on the windows, and a size-zero stewardess slicing up a pot roast in the galley. I hate to burst anyone's bubble, but those old Pan Am Clippers from vintage posters we romanticize used to fall out of the sky quite a bit. It's all too common to overhear someone complaining about how "long" the flight is from New York to Los Angeles. Had any of us been born just a few hundred years earlier, a trip to California would have consisted of a six-month ride in a bumpy-ass covered wagon. Business class could be defined as not being scalped by Indians or dying from dysentery.

It was only 105 years ago, on a windy stretch of beach in North Carolina, that Orville and Wilbur Wright launched the first powered aircraft: the fragile-looking *Wright Flyer I*. The plane, which flew for a meager twelve seconds, fundamentally changed the world. It's impossible to know the extent to which the brothers envisioned the evolution of their invention, but I can only assume they never dreamed of Richard Branson. Among many other things, the advent of flight and the eventual age of the jumbo jet have turned the world into a much smaller place. With the unveiling of Boeing's long-haul 777, any two cities on earth can now hypothetically be connected by a single flight. That we've taken this interconnectedness for granted is nothing short of a sin. So stop complaining, drink your Bloody Mary, and enjoy the free DirecTV.

We are in dire need of a public relations campaign for travel. I'm not talking about splashy commercials for Carnival Cruises or full-page magazine ads for Sandals resorts; we've got plenty of those, thank you very much. Nearly the entire vacation industry is hell-bent on the notion that travel is a purely escapist enterprise — that the sole purpose of leaving one's country is to drink daiquiris and plummet down a waterslide with a big, dumb grin. Why isn't there a marketing campaign that extols the innate virtues of wandering?

The real hindrance is that we've forgotten how to travel — or, more important, we've ceased to remember that it's good for us. In Europe, aristocratic youth were once encouraged to undertake the "Grand Tour," a rite of passage that involved hopscotching across the continent, experiencing the legacy of the Renaissance and the influences of the Classical world. Hundreds of years later, the cultural tradition endures in much more bohemian packaging. It's called a "gap year." Tens of thousands of backpackers take a year off before or after college to expose themselves to foreign cultures. More than an extended vacation, gap years are considered a critical part of any well-rounded student's résumé. In America, most people would probably guess that a gap year is an annual jeans sale at the mall.

The experience of leaving one's homeland can be psychologically profound. Travel illuminates a strange dichotomy of scale. When we stand in the shadows of empire, before solemn, ancient temples, we feel the enormity of human history wash over us and are humbled by its magnitude. But, paradoxically, the world is also revealed to us as strangely small and universal. It is impossible to watch that old familiar moon rise up over Hong Kong Harbor and not be struck dumb by the idea that the same soft light is shining down on Burbank, California. To think that when we look west over the misty cliffs of Moher in Ireland, someone on a beach in Cape Cod, Massachusetts, is looking back. In an instant, we can observe the world expand and contract in one seemingly contradictory motion.

To that dangerously expanding group of xenophobic Americans who seems content cleaving only to the familiar embrace of the United States, I contend that you will, on some level, forever feel unfulfilled. Seeing the world is a prerequisite to understanding one's place in it. After all, nearly every corner of this country is rife with invitations that beckon us back to foreign shores. Look around. We're illuminated by the torchlight of a giant Roman goddess in New York Harbor. Our currency is adorned with arcane pyramids, and half the days of the week are named after Viking gods. We are derivative, the star-spangled orphans of a hundred civilizations before us. And, like all orphans, we should yearn to understand from whence we came.

Don't get me wrong. I may be an ex-pat by profession, but I'm also a proud American. Admiring the Constitution without treading on the ancestral English homeland of our founding fathers, however, seems folly. How can some of my countrymen be so afraid of the outside world when our very democracy was born on the faraway streets of Athens, and considering our great diaspora from the vast savannahs of Africa?

Finally, yes, travel is a hell of a lot of fun. The Club Med ads are right. There's little in our domestic routines that compares to swimming in Caribbean waters. Not to mention racing motorcycles through the back alleys of Vietnam, dining on a rooftop in Marrakech, or waking up under the canopy of the Amazon. By staying home, we're missing a grand opportunity afforded to us by those glimmering silver birds in the sky. The "golden age" of travel is right now. Jetting is no longer just for the jet set; it's for everyone. The truth is that travel changes us, irrevocably, and mostly for the better. It can nourish the best parts of ourselves like nothing else. Travel broadens our perspective, adds texture to our lives, and makes us more interesting at cocktail parties.

So, please. I'm begging you. Go away. Often.

20: Something in the Fog

Every once in a while our overnight investigations on
Destination Truth turn magical; under a canopy of stars, the
serenity of nature reveals itself, and I'm convinced I have the
best job in the world. This is not one of those times. This is the
time when I almost freeze to death.

Our tale unfolds within the fiberglass confines of a small
boat caught in the dangerous embrace of fog. Through this
translucent blanket of icy, arctic air, I finally see with my own
eyes what others before me have seen. A monster.

We've arrived on Iceland's shores looking for adventure,
something that this mysterious island is more than willing to
provide. It is, quite simply, a geologic wonderland. A gurgling,
steaming, hissing isle prone to mercurial weather and explosive
disasters. Perpetually locked in a battle between the forces of
fire and ice, this has long been a place of legends.

To the Greeks it was "Ultima Thule," a distant island
beyond the borders of the known world. By the tenth century,
Norse ships had navigated the treacherous Norwegian Sea and
discovered what they called the "Land of Snow." Once ashore,
they discovered deafening waterfalls, volcanic peaks, and the

largest ice cap in Europe. But Viking rule was as tempestuous
as the land itself, and it would take another millennium before
stability and eventual independence emerged. Today, the more
than thousand-year-old city of Reykjavík has evolved from a
primitive Norse settlement to a cosmopolitan capital. Known
for pulsing nightlife, charming hotels, and posh thermal
springs, it is a shockingly overpriced but unarguably worth-it
destination.

Outside the confines of the city, though, the rest of
Iceland seems positively prehistoric. Our jeep doubles as a
time machine and we leave the modern city, watching as chic
bars and souvenir shops are replaced by soaring cliffs and misty
waterfalls. Eventually, the road skirts along the behemoth
Vatnajökull Glacier, an amoebic flow of ice that covers nearly
10 percent of the entire country. It's instantly recognizable
to fans of Christopher Nolan's *Batman Begins*, in which it
effortlessly passed for the most remote corner of the Himalayas.

Our crew is rounded out by Erin Ryder, or just "Ryder,"
as she's known on the show. Ryder has appeared in probably a
third of all *D.T.* episodes, and though she sometimes startles
easily on camera, she's actually tough as nails and one hell of
a copilot. She curses like a sailor, takes crap from nobody, and
if you punched her in the abs you'd probably break your hand.
My kind of girl.

It takes more than a day for all of us to reach the edge of
Lake Lagarfljót, which comes partially into view as we arrive at
a small airport in the adjacent town of Egilsstaðir. We hop on
board a Cessna and loft up over the forests to get a better look
at the water. The lake is narrow, only about a mile and a half
across. But what it lacks in width it makes up for in length. I

peer in both directions from the aircraft cockpit but can't make out either end of the more-than-thirty-mile-long basin.

A dusty page on one of Iceland's historic annals reads: "Year 1345: Hump seen rising out of the waters of Lake Lagarfljót." Over the following centuries, more sightings of a serpentine, worm-like creature accumulated and were recorded. Eventually, belief in a nearly unpronounceable monster known as Lagarfljótsormur took hold. We've traveled to the lake to investigate the most recent sightings of the massive beast.

Back on the ground, we spend the afternoon interviewing eyewitnesses and experts in the region. A lifelong resident and forest ranger vividly remembers seeing a long, black shape moving along the surface of the water. A woman recounts the day that she and her classmates spied the animal while on a field trip. A ferry captain who has navigated these waters for decades attests to several occasions when his vessel's sophisticated onboard sonar system imaged something huge in the depths of the lake. To his amazement, the object even changed direction, moving against the prevailing current. All of the eyewitnesses put the animal at more than sixty feet long. A freshwater biologist informs us that the largest living fauna in these waters is a trout. Hardly the behemoth worm monster residents claim to have seen.

We aggregate the sightings, identify the most prominent area, and mount a scuba-diving investigation. The enterprise is a mess from the start. Iceland's frosty waters aren't exactly a diver's paradise, so the only dry suits we're able to source are about three times too small for my producer Casey and me. It takes a bottle of baby powder and the combined effort of the entire crew to squeeze us into the Lilliputian neoprene outfits. By the time I pull my hood on, I feel as though my eyeballs are going to shoot out of my head.

The surface is ice-cold, and conditions beneath the waves are worse. About ten feet down, the water turns to coffee-colored silt, and Casey and I lose sight of each other immediately. I clumsily descend as less and less light filters through the darkening water. Eventually, my faceplate shows only liquid blackness. In the murk, something moves by me. It could be an animal or perhaps just a piece of debris. I'm basically blind. The only chance I have of finding the creature down here is to be eaten by it. It also doesn't help that our underwater communication system is crippled by the muddy conditions, unable to transmit our messages to the rest of the team onshore. It's a dangerous waste of time. We ascend to the surface, where Casey and I paddle back to land, blue-lipped and shivering.

We opt to refocus our efforts topside. Our base camp is established in the area where the majority of firsthand accounts have been reported. We park our Land Rover on the beach of an isolated cove to unload our gear. It's getting colder, so we gather up some driftwood along the shore to fuel a fire. We've sourced two boats from locals that are, per our instructions, tied up along the cove's simple dock: one small boat with an engine and an even smaller white rowboat.

About an hour before sunset, I want to take a few of the team members on a scouting run in the motorboat to get a lay of the land. Our camera operator, Gabe, audio technician, Richie, and paramedic, Jarrod, all climb aboard while Ryder, Casey, and Erica stay onshore. I'm rushing, since it's going to be nighttime soon, and I hate piloting boats in unfamiliar waters after dark. In my haste, I forget my compass and GPS unit in the Land Rover, an oversight I'll be bitterly replaying in my mind later.

Placing my foot on the motor, I yank the ripcord, and the engine fires up right away. On the distant opposing shore, I can discern several vertical cliffs interrupted by rolling fields and the occasional beach. Looking to my left and to my right, I see only more lake. It's like an immense sliver of water, serpentine in its own right. We get about halfway to the other side, and I look back, narrowing my eyes in the failing light, trying to make out our Land Rover and tiny camp on the beach behind us. *This is going to be a bitch after dark*, I think to myself.

I'm not sure when I first notice the wisps of cloud tumbling down over the cliffs, but I do manage to misinterpret their significance entirely. To me, the thickening sky is a portent of rain. Nothing more. Just after eight p.m. I call Ryder.

"Josh to base camp. Come in, base camp."

"Hey, Josh," Ryder calls back on the radio. "Go ahead for base camp."

"Continuing my survey of the lake. Chop is picking up a little bit and so is the wind. Clouds are coming in, so make sure everything is secure to be dry over there," I warn, looking up at the sky.

"We'll do some prep work, and you guys take care," she says.

"Copy that. No sign of a worm monster yet, but it's cold as hell out here."

While Ryder makes preparations for a rainstorm that will never arrive, I continue down the spine of the lake. As long as we have a little light, I don't want to abandon our efforts. Shortly after, my engine quits. A quick check of gas canisters and fuel line reveal nothing amiss. I let it sit for a minute and then start her back up, dismissing a vague instinct to take the boat ashore.

By nine p.m. it's dark. Casey calls in on the radio to tell me that a mist is beginning to shroud some of the outlying infrared cameras that he's monitoring at camp. As we speak over the walkie, one by one his cameras turn white. I can see what he sees. From the center of the lake, both shores are rapidly fading from view, cloaked behind fingers of fog.

Ten p.m. The temperature has dropped precipitously since the sun went down, and our onboard thermometer reads only 22 degrees Fahrenheit. I've throttled back to a crawl, since I can hardly see where I'm going. The opposing banks have vanished. The thermal imager is able to make them out, but only slightly. The water is now dead calm, and the air is eerily silent. Jarrod comments that we should make sure to remember which side of the lake we started on, at which point everyone in the boat silently points in a different direction. It's funny, really. We all have a good laugh about it, although I'm starting to feel uneasy.

The mercury is dropping by the minute, and none of us is prepared for an entire night out here. We aren't wearing enough layers and only have a few spare tapes and batteries for our cameras. Clearly it's time to regroup with the rest of our team. Not able to reach a consensus on which shore is ours, we work out a sensible plan: take the boat to one of the shores, visually mark a point on land, and then run the boat up and down the banks for a half mile in each direction. If we don't find the camp, we'll return to the marked position and pilot the boat across the lake to repeat the process on the other side.

We steer into the nothingness. It's a disorienting experience.

If it weren't for the water splashing off the sides of the boat, I'd swear we were stationary. Then the opaque fog in front of us suddenly goes dark, like someone has pulled a curtain down over the world. It takes me a moment to realize that the blackness I see is a massive cliff face rising up nearly one hundred feet and stretching out in either direction. I drop us into reverse and throw my hand down on the throttle, backing off from the encroaching wall. Turning the boat 90 degrees, I begin to follow the land. Since the cliff is featureless, we decide to carry on until we can find a natural marker. The wall passes by silently and eventually disintegrates into a cove. I idle the boat. In front of us, an empty beach and a listing white rowboat that sits half submerged at a broken dock. I shiver. The cove looks exactly like our base camp, and the rowboat is identical to the one we left onshore. It's an uncomfortable coincidence.

With the cove as a marker, we steam along the shore in both directions. I radio Casey and tell him to point the Land Rover toward the water and turn the high beams on. He does. We see nothing. I ask Casey and Ryder to yell, and we listen intently. A faint echo of their voices ekes out of the mist and reverberates off the cliffs. They don't sound close by, and we assume that we're on the wrong side of the lake. We make every effort to set a direct course across, and I motor away from land. With over a mile and a half of blankness, the crossing seems to take forever. When we reach the center of the lake, a quiet seriousness sets in amongst the crew. I drive as straight as I can, looking back at our boat wake to make sure it doesn't bend. Finally, Jarrod calls out, "Slow down! Land!"

I coax the engine back into neutral and stand up to look over the bow. What I see makes my stomach sink like a rock.

We've arrived in an empty cove. A white, partially sunken rowboat creaks in the still night air. "How . . ." someone starts, and then trails off.

I've read about this phenomenon, of course. I just never thought I'd be caught in an example of it. Without a fixed point, traveling in a straight line is all but impossible. The tiniest errors in navigational judgment cause massive drift in direction. Without a star or the moon to guide us, we've come full circle. As I run my gloved hand over my head, I feel brittle icicles in my hair. We're starting to freeze. It's just before midnight. The thermometer reads 18 degrees.

We make another attempt. The cove recedes, and the fog happily takes us back in. When we do find land again, it's in the form of another anonymous cliff. We turn and run parallel, only to be returned to the same damned place. There are a few frightening images that cling to the back of my mind from my years of travel, and the sight of this lonely beach and derelict rowboat is one of them. It feels like a trick. A sickening piece of witchcraft. *Fair is foul, and foul is fair: / Hover through the fog and filthy air.*

After three failed attempts we decide to go ashore in the cove. We raise the engine and beach the boat. While the crew struggles up a steep hill, I secure the boat anchor on land. Part of me expects the boat to vanish altogether as soon as I turn around. We walk for a while. At the crest of the hill we're greeted by a bleak landscape. No road. No welcoming chimney smoke from a farm, no telephone poles. Nothing. Just fog and field. After all, this is one of the most sparsely populated countries in the world. I look down at my feet in despair. "Back to the boat, guys."

In the middle of the lake, it occurs to me that even though we heard Casey and Ryder earlier, I have no idea how long it took for their voices to reach us. We cut our engine, and I ask them to call out again. This time with their walkie on. "HELLO!" I hear them yell through my radio. I immediately begin counting. "One . . . two . . . three . . . four . . . five . . . six . . ." Nothing. " . . . seven . . . eight . . . nine . . . ten . . . eleven . . . twel—" Suddenly a faint "HELLOOOO!" I realize now that the steep walls are acting like sounding boards, carrying their words along. They could be anywhere on either shore. With only a quarter of a tank of gas left and the temperature now hovering at 11 degrees, we can't afford to be in the middle of the lake any longer. I decide to take the boat to one of the shores and just drive along it until we run out of fuel (at which point I suppose we'll begin a new life as half-frozen Icelandic gypsies).

The point of this story isn't about the fog, though. It isn't about the boat in the fog. It isn't even about the freezing people in the boat or the despair that overtook us. It's about the water and what we see. By two thirty a.m. we're out of ideas and running low on patience. And then we see it. Everyone sees it at the exact same moment. A shape. A long, dark, sinewy thing gliding across the glassy water behind our boat. Everyone stands up to look. It makes no noise, nor does it fully breach the surface. But it's there. Like a silent submarine. A V-shaped wake spreads out and laps against our hull. The boat rocks back and forth above the disturbance. And then it's gone. Silence. Glassy water. Fog.

The sighting takes a second to sink in but then hits like a kick to the ribs. Everyone onboard is suddenly talking, the cold banished by fierce debate over what we just saw. I start running the boat in circles, looking down into the black water for any signs of movement. Our walkies are dying, but I raise Casey long enough to excitedly tell him to get out in the rowboat with Ryder and activate the sonar equipment. I also advise him not to lose sight of land.

Despite our best efforts and another few hours of drifting over the area of the sighting, nothing else emerges. It's gone. The fog lifts at five a.m., revealing all the puzzle pieces of the lake that I'd been trying to fit together in the dark. The cliffs and coves and fields interlock once more, and I can see that while we've drifted farther from camp than I imagined, it won't take long to get back. We head for our small cove, smiling at the sight of a working dock and a rowboat floating safely on the water. By the time we tie up, we've been on the water for more than nine hours. Our fuel reserves are nearly depleted, and our ice-caked thermometer reads 8 degrees.

Everyone heads back to the lodge to get warm and eat a much-needed meal. We replay the night over and over, joking about getting lost and blaming one another for having a terrible sense of direction. We feverishly compare descriptions of the mystery creature in Lake Lagarfljót. But beneath the jokes and merry conversation, there's discomfort. The truth is, we were scared out in that boat and perhaps luckier than we deserved. But mostly there's an unspoken fear that we can't and never will understand our sighting. In the end, we are merely another entry. One of hundreds added to the yellowing pages of a historical log.

"Year 2008. Americans see something in the fog."

CASE FILE: *MARINE MONSTERS*

NAMES: Nessie, Champ, Ogopogo, Issie, Van Lake Monster, Nahuelito, Pinatubo Monster, Icelandic Worm Monster, Phaya Naga, Mamlambo, Ri, mermaid, Lusca, Tarasque.

DESCRIPTION: Depictions of sea monsters are as varied as the seven seas themselves. Often described as long-necked beasts or multi-humped snakes, these creatures fall primarily into three categories: descendants of prehistoric reptiles, sea serpents, and mermaids.

LOCATIONS: These slippery creatures are found worldwide and in every type of body of water imaginable, from endless oceans to tiny ponds (not to mention those alligators in the sewers). Anyplace you go swimming and feel something brush up against your leg, chances are there's someone who'd have you believe it's a monster.

STATUS: Aquatic creatures make up a sizable slice of the cryptozoological pie, probably because 70 percent of the planet is concealed by liquid, and the technology needed to explore the underwater world has only recently come of age. Our oceans, rivers, and lakes have always been a source of great intrigue and adventure, and the belief that unknown monsters lurk just below the surface only adds to the narrative. After all, who among us hasn't spotted ripples on a quiet lake or waves in a calm sea and asked himself, <u>What was that?</u>

    Scotland's infamous Loch Ness Monster is the granddame of all aquatic cryptids. With a legend that dates back centuries, Nessie is to monsters what Coca-Cola is to refreshing beverages. She and her aquatic ilk are allegedly just the resilient descendants of extinct prehistoric reptiles such as the plesiosaur. It's easy for people to believe in the possibility of these creatures, since they did actually exist at one time. However, modern evidence is primarily anecdotal, supported only by the occasional grainy photograph. Several iconic photos once presented as proof of the beast's existence have since been revealed as hoaxes. The propagation of lake monster myths has also become a cottage industry in tourist-hungry towns all around the world. In the United States alone, there's a Bessie, Gnessie, Chessie, Messie, Altie, Whitey, Pressie, Tessie, Hodgee, and Slimy Slim.

VERDICT: Reports of lake monsters are compelling mostly because they tend to be backed by more eyewitness testimony than any other type of cryptozoological entity. There are hundreds upon hundreds of people who believe they have seen these animals. Although tales of sea serpents date back to antiquity, historic sightings are most likely cases of mistaken identity. In the early centuries of nautical exploration, glimpses of yet-to-be-cataloged oceanic fauna were easy inspiration for these types of stories.

Mermaids are likely misidentified manatees—although a sea cow doesn't bear much resemblance to a beautiful woman, does it? What probably happened is that, after months at sea, a lonely sailor fondled a manatee, got busted, and then claimed he was

seduced by an irresistible sea nymph. The legend
of the mermaid: a far-fetched, drunken alibi gone
horribly wrong.

The stumbling block to these types of stories
is scientific. Every animal needs what is called a
"breeding population" in order to survive. Basically,
there can't be just one Nessie. There have to be
enough Nessies in the lake so that the creatures
can reproduce without inbreeding or failing to find
a mate. With multiple gigantic creatures living
in these confined bodies of water, one might
expect sightings to occur hourly (especially since
plesiosaurs are reptiles and would need to surface
for air to survive).

That being said, our oceans are proving to be a
nearly limitless source of undiscovered creatures.
Advances in deepwater exploration are opening the
door to an unseen world, and literally thousands of
new species are being documented each year. Is
it possible that a population of large sea monsters
is living in the deepest regions of our oceans?
Perhaps. It's unquestionably more likely than the
existence of Slimy Slim in Payette Lake, Idaho.

21: What the Monsters Taught Me

As this goes to print, I've filmed four and a half seasons of *Destination Truth* and investigated more than eighty individual stories, a fact that sneaks up and surprises me even now. I'm within a stone's throw of traveling to a hundred countries, and I've broken bread with individuals from more cultures than I can count. It seems like I should have something to say for myself, some epiphanic revelations after four years of professional monster hunting.

I've certainly learned how to be a better traveler. I can pass through an airport security line like a ghost (in case you're interested, the correct order of objects on the X-ray belt is shoes, accessories, bag, then computer). I've learned to sit tight and be the last person off an airplane, since baggage claim carousels are a tiny circle of hell. I've learned that the *Thousand Places to See Before You Die* book is a great read unless you travel for a living, in which case it only serves to remind you that you're just about ready to die. I am now a frequent-flyer program savant, a packing guru, and a connoisseur of questionable roadside bathrooms. Oh, and I've also learned how to drive in reverse while ducking from arrows.

Hunting monsters has also provided me with a hard-knocks education in television hosting and producing. Since I began working on *Destination Truth*, the Syfy Channel has generously seen fit to utilize me in other, varied capacities. In 2007, I began my now four-year tenure as the host of *Ghost Hunters Live* on Halloween night. Then, in 2010, I was fortunate enough to host the one hundredth episode of *Ghost Hunters* from historic Studio 8H in 30 Rockefeller Center. The key to hosting live television, I've come to know, is that the only way to make it look easy is to remember that it isn't and to prepare accordingly.

But much more important, I've learned that most of us are a lot luckier than we acknowledge. To see children suffering from malnutrition or to visit countries where personal liberties are few is to know gratitude for whatever cosmic fluke granted many of us brighter circumstances.

I'm often asked if I think that the people we interview are crazy. Almost universally, I do not. Are there crazy people out there associated with the types of stories we investigate? Sure, although most of them don't know they're crazy. You think Norman Bates knew he was crazy? No, of course not. He just cleaned up that shower, put on his mother's nightgown, and made himself a pot roast. I've learned that it's best not to engage with people who peddle conspiracy theories, hawk Chupacabra key chains, or believe that *Invasion of the Body Snatchers* is an allegory for immigration reform. Instead, we stick to earnest accounts and try to tell people's stories fairly, with humor and enthusiasm.

The frequent question of whether the creatures we look for are real is also frustrating, since I've come to believe it misses the point. The salient fact is that the *stories* about the creatures are real. Many of them are the continuations of oral traditions stretching back thousands of years. Between the lines of these legends is a code, a subtle language that informs us about beliefs, values, and the social psychology of a group of people. And in some cases, yes, they just might point us toward an undiscovered creature or a legitimate phenomenon.

Take the Cyclops. It would be easy to dismiss this visually challenged cave dweller as merely a character of ancient fiction, nothing more. In reality, it may well be that the legend, included in Homer's epic *The Odyssey*, has roots in reality. The ancients encountered fossilized pygmy elephant bones in caves throughout the Mediterranean. Intriguingly, the nasal cavity of the skulls looks alarmingly like a single eye socket. In an effort to make sense of these unsettlingly large bones (and with no knowledge of elephants), it's possible that locals interpreted the remains as a race of giant, single-eyed humanoids. The notion that some of the most enduring creature stories of all time may be an early version of archaeology is fascinating stuff. It goes to show that even the most outlandish of legends is worth consideration.

This speaks to something universal in the human condition. We all want to understand the world around us. Man has an undeniable desire to explore and an inherent need to rationalize. The ancients crafted poetic myths to bring order and context to the universe, and the tradition continues to this day with every Bigfoot sighting or paranormal encounter. We cannot bear for our most mysterious experiences to remain unexplained. I've therefore learned, above all, that every story has worth, since a person takes the time to tell it. The key is to listen.

22: Home

Everything feels sore. I slip off my boots, stretch out my toes,
and let out a deep sigh. My arms are sunburned and dry, there's
a gash on my finger that needs rewrapping, and I can't wait to
change this shirt. I've been wearing it for days. Somewhere in
the luggage hold below, my pack is stuffed with damp socks,
muddy cargo pants, and various other distressed pieces of my
wardrobe, which probably stink to high hell.

Outside the window I see nothing but clouds and
moonlight. I glance at the map on the seat-back screen in front
of me. We're cruising at 34,000 feet, more than six hundred
miles per hour. It's hard to believe. Just inches beyond the
cozy silence of this Boeing 747 jet, the thin and frigid air is
screaming by. From here, though, just across the threshold,
the silent majesty of it all is simply meditative. I've studied
this lunar view a thousand times. It usually means I'm going
somewhere new. I instinctively associate it with anticipation of
the unknown. But tonight I'm going home.

This flight, my eighty-first this year, marks the last leg
of this season's overseas production. The crew has scattered

to the wind: a few will remain overseas, others are returning
to Los Angeles, New York, and small towns in between. I'm
fantasizing about a crackling fire and snow falling outside
the windows of my family home in Massachusetts. The plane
corrects course slightly and momentarily bucks in the strong
headwinds outside. I watch the tiny animated plane on the
screen in front of me shift direction. I know that by the time the
sun breaks up through the clouds, we'll be landing in Boston.
I slip off my wristwatch, adjust the bevel to U.S. Eastern
Standard Time, and smile — it's Christmas Eve.

Despite my cultivating ease with unfamiliar places and
an ability to sleep in just about any uncomfortable corner of
free space on earth, sometimes my brain forgets that this is my
day-to-day life. I wake up sometimes and don't know where I
am. It happens more and more these days. Recently, I came to
in an unfamiliar hotel room, suddenly overcome with panic.
Clutching for the lamp, I smashed a glass on the bedside table
and grasped at the only thing I could find: a notepad with a
Chinese letterhead. I stared at the characters in horror, tears
in my eyes, unable to recall anything about my circumstances.
And then, it hit me. I'm in Beijing. We're filming *Destination
Truth*. All is well.

We all fundamentally crave familiarity. It's hardwired in us.
For me, most days lack this stability. I don't know much about
where I'm headed. Hell, I don't even know where I'm going to
sleep most nights until I walk through the door. But tonight, I
have the great comfort of knowing that my father will be picking
me up at the airport in his truck, my mother is working on a
delectable turkey dinner, and cold ocean waves are crashing
methodically outside my childhood bedroom window.

Travel does not exist without home. They are inseparably married. If we never return to the place we started, we would just be wandering, lost. Home is a reflecting surface, a place to measure our growth and enrich us after being infused with the outside world. More than anything, though, it's a safe haven.

Over the last two seasons I've received a steady stream of e-mails, letters, tweets, and Facebook messages from people inquiring about how to get my job. To those interested in becoming a "cryptozoologist," I would gently redirect you toward study in the sciences of zoology, biology, paleontology, or archaeology. To those who want to know how to become a full-time traveler, the short answer is: Just do it. Exploration and adventure are seldom backed by anything other than curious individuals with a desire to experience the unknown and cast a little light into uncharted corners of the world. Opportunities for employment will follow. I promise.

I never argue with people who tell me that I've got "the best job in the world" because I largely agree with them. But there is a price for accepting the position. My closet has been reduced to a single fifty-pound bag, and every night ends on a borrowed bed, or sometimes just a wooden floor. Most important, the job requires a terrible downsizing of family and friends, all of whom are listed at the bottom of a flight itinerary for much of the calendar year.

I read books by other career travelers and discern a sort of conflict that's familiar to me now. It's a melancholy felt by all professional pilgrims that simmers just beneath the joy of never having to conform. To live in motion is to always be caught between worlds, a liminal existence. I slow down just long enough to fall in love with a place, yet never long enough to feel like I belong.

But whatever considerations have come with the job, it's all been unarguably worth it. Along with having the great privilege of globetrotting for a living, I get the unique opportunity to share our many destinations with viewers around the world. One of my great hopes is that the show excites other people to travel. I can assure you that in nearly every country on earth, there are warm, hospitable, and fascinating people who want to share their stories and cultures with anyone who makes the effort to come and listen. And don't worry: home will be waiting for you right where you left it.

Outside the window I can see nothing but white vapor now. We've descended and are flying through the cloud line toward North America. Below me, stretching out for 24,000 miles, is the vast, ephemeral equator of the earth. I feel as though I've only scratched the surface down there. I strain my eyes through the mist, eager to make out something below, and wide-eyed at the prospect of adventure on the horizon.

Acknowledgments

I would like to warmly acknowledge the following people: my mother and father for raising me adventurously; Ray Bradbury for sparking a young kid's imagination; Gloria Tanner and the late Tony Cornish for your mentorship; Neil Mandt for giving me a career in the first place; Brad Kuhlman for keeping it alive; the *D.T.* crew for taking on the hardest job in television; Rob Swartz for nurturing the series in its infancy; Dave Howe, Mark Stern, Alan Seiffert, and everyone from Syfy who encouraged me to take this project on; Hallie Gnatovich for your endless encouragement, patient editing, and driving 2,042 miles round-trip to Santa Fe just so I could type in the passenger seat; Steven Spielberg for every movie you made before 1994 and for four of the movies you've made since then; Diet Coke for always being there; Maura Teitelbaum from Abrams Artists and the good people at Simon & Schuster for putting up with my many disappearing acts; and, finally, the loyal fans of *Destination Truth*, who ride along the bumpy roads with us week after week, and without whom my passport would have far fewer stamps.

Cheers.
Josh